Religion

Titles of Interest from St. Augustine's Press

The Two Eyes of Spinoza and Other Esssays on Philosophers (St. Augustine's Press)

Husserl and the Search for Certitude (St. Augustine's Press)

Zbigniew Janowski, *Augustinian-Cartesian Index*

Rémi Brague, *Eccentric Culture: A Theory of Western Civilization*

Francisco Suarez, *On Creation, Conservation, & Concurrence: Metaphysical Disputations 20–22*

Francisco Suarez, *Metaphysical Demonstration to the Existence of God*

John of St. Thomas, *Introduction to the Summa Theologiae of Thomas Aquinas*

William of Ockham, *Ockham's Theory of Terms: Part I of the Summa Logicae*

William of Ockham, *Ockham's Theory of Propositions: Part II of the Summa Logicae*

Roger Bacon, Roger *Bacon's Philosophy of Nature. Translation of De multiplicatione specierum and De speculis comburentibus*

Roger Scruton, *An Intelligent Person's Guide to Modern Culture*

Roger Scruton, *On Hunting*

Roger Scruton, *Art and Imagination: A Study in the Philosophy of Mind*

Roger Scruton, *Aesthetic Understanding*

Roger Scruton, *The Meaning of Conservatism*

Josef Pieper, *In Tune with the World: A Theory of Festivity*

Josef Pieper, *Happiness and Contemplation*

Josef Pieper, *The Christian Idea of Man*

Josef Pieper, *Death and Immortality*

Josef Pieper, *Scholasticism: Personalities and Problems*

Josef Pieper, *The Silence of St. Thomas*

Mario Enrique Sacchi, *The Apocalypse of Being: The Esoteric Gnosis of Martin Heidegger*

Friedrich Nietzsche, *On the Future of Our Educational Institutions*

Friedrich Nietzsche, *Prefaces to Unwritten Works*

René Girard, *A Theater of Envy: William Shakespeare*

Stanley Rosen, *The Question of Being: A Reversal of Heidegger*

Stanley Rosen, *Nihilism: A Philosophical Essay*

Richard A. Watson, *Solipsism: The Ultimate Empirical Theory of Human Existence*

Étienne Gilson, *Theology and the Cartesian Doctrine of Freedom*

James V. Schall, *The Classical Momenet: Seleeted Essays on Knowledge and Its Pleasures*

Religion
If There Is No God . . .
On God, the Devil, Sin and Other Worries of the so-called Philosophy of Religion

Leszek Kolakowski

ST. AUGUSTINE'S PRESS
South Bend, Indiana

Manufactured in the United States of America.

3 4 5 6   20 19 18 17 16 15

Library of Congress Cataloging in Publication Data
Kolakowski, Leszek.
    [Religion, if there is no God]
    Religion : if there is no God : on God, the Devil, sin, and other
    worries of the so-called philosophy of religion /
    Leszek Kolakowski.
       p. cm.
    Originally published: Religion, if there is no God. New York:
`   Oxford University Press, 1982.
    Includes index.
    ISBN 1-890318-87-6 (alk. paper)
    I. Religion – Philosophy. I. Title.
BL51.K64 2000
210 – dc21   00-062618

∞ *The paper used in this publication meets the minimum requirements of the*
American National Standard for Information Sciences – Permanence of Paper for
Printed Materials, ANSI Z39.48-1984.

Contents

Acknowledgements

This book has been written in a language pretending to be somewhat similar to English. Professor Frank Kermode and his wife, Anita, proved, alas, that the similarity was much more remote than the author had imagined. They made a Herculean effort to reshape this text into something an English reader can look at without shuddering (not for linguistic reasons, that is). The author's gratitude is as immense as their toil.

What it is about

This book deals with what is usually called the philosophy of religion. I am never sure what religion, let alone philosophy is, but whatever religion is, it includes the history of gods, men and the universe. Therefore the title, *Religion*, with its all-encompassing pretensions, could only compete with such works as Quine's *On What There Is* or Sartre's *Being and Nothingness* (probably the most comprehensive title ever devised).

Still, I cannot avoid using the word 'religion'. Mircea Eliade, to whom my understanding of the problems arising in comparative religious studies owes a great deal, regrets that there is no better word to cover what he calls 'the experience of the Sacred'. And yet it does not seem that any neologism would be helpful. In the investigation of human affairs no concepts at our disposal can be defined with perfect precision and in this respect 'religion' is in no worse a position than 'art', 'society', 'culture', 'history', 'politics', 'science', 'language' and countless other words. Any definition of religion has to be arbitrary to a certain extent, and no matter how scrupulously we try to make it conform to the actual usage of the word in current speech, many people will feel that our definition covers too much or too little or both. We have become aware of the existence, in various civilizations, of an incalculable number of myths, rituals, beliefs and magical acts, and it is not immediately clear which of them deserve to be called 'religious'. Indeed anthropologists, in the study of mythologies, often manage very well without distinguishing between religious and non-religious tales. The absence of sharply drawn conceptual limits results less from our logical ineptitude than from the nature of the reality under scrutiny. It is largely our interest that determines which among various forms of behaviour, believing and feeling we consider essential to the phenomenon of religion as we know it from experience and books. The important thing is to maintain a distinction between the way in which we delineate, more or less arbitrarily, our scope of inquiry, and our inevitably controversial explanatory statements about the function of religious life. If, like Rudolf Otto and Mircea Eliade, we hold that the experience of the sacred is peculiar to and indeed constitutive in analysing the religious phenomenon, we encounter the problem that the word 'sacred' is often used seriously and with strong commitment by people who otherwise consider themselves non-religious. Thus the field may seem larger than current speech would allow; nevertheless such a definition is good enough to mark off a very important area of reflection. If, on the other hand, we try to proceed socratically and look for a set of specific beliefs that no known religion fails to include, we risk being disappointed and finding that the set is empty. As soon as a personal god is introduced as a candidate for the position of such a constant, it is invariably objected that such an enormously important phenomenon as Buddhism has been left aside. This is awkward, of course, but again there is nothing empirically or logically wrong in focusing attention on beliefs which include the idea of a personal god and thus in regarding Buddhism as a metaphysical and moral wisdom, rather than as a religion in the full sense.

Various definitions are thus permissible; however those which imply that religion is 'nothing but' an instrument of secular – social or psychological – needs (e.g. that its meaning is reducible to its function in social integration) are illicit; they are empirical statements (false, I believe) and may not be admitted in advance as parts of a definition.

Nor is there any common agreement about what is meant by 'the philosophy of religion'. In the Anglo-Saxon philosophical parlance its task is to investigate the truth-claims of religious beliefs and this includes the analysis of concepts specific to religious language as it is used in theological and philosophical tradition; this task is contrasted with anthropological and psychological inquiry which explores the various ways in which myths and rites operate in human life, what their social, intellectual and emotional functions are, and how they change or die under the impact of social transformation. In the German, Italian and, in general, 'continental' tradition, the topics designated by the term 'philosophy of religion' correspond only marginally with those which come under the same heading in Anglo-American usage. Especially since Hegel, Schelling, Schleiermacher and the romantics, philosophical reflection on religion has been concentrated on its meaning in historical processes, and on the way in which various civilizations or mankind as a whole have expressed through religious symbols the perception of their destiny. Philosophy of religion appeared as an important, even a constitutive, part of the philosophy of history, the latter being understood less as the epistemological analysis of historical statements than as speculation on the global sense, goals and guiding principles of historical processes. Perhaps the most outstanding recent work in this area is Karl Jaspers's *Der Philosophische Glaube angesichts der Offenbarung* (1962).

The advantage of the analytical approach is that a scholar may spin out his tale without any interest in, or any acquaintance with, the history of religion and without knowing the cultural contexts of the various attempts to cope with ultimate questions. Its disadvantage, on the other hand, consists in that more often than not the philosopher discusses problems which, though perfectly valid in themselves, are very remote from the real worries of both religious and irreligious people. Within the analytical framework religion is conceived of as a collection of statements about God, Providence, immortality, angels and related subjects, while the concept of truth is usually taken over from other chapters of philosophy without being subjected to the question whether and how it is modified when used in the field of religious symbols. On the other hand, those who indulge in historiosophical meditation are usually more knowledgeable in historical matters and more sensitive to the cultural relativity of religious concepts, yet less rigorous in their analytical work and in clarifying the abstract categories they employ. To combine the virtues of both kinds of an analysis would be a counsel of perfection; to combine the vices of both is easier.

Though in the following pages I am more interested in beliefs than in rituals – and I leave aside the time-honoured quarrel about their respective priority – I take the act of worship as unremovable and intrinsic to any description of the phenomenon of religion. The socially established worship of the eternal reality: this formulation comes perhaps closest to what I have in mind when talking of religion. It does not pretend to be a 'definition' and I am not sure that it fits in with what is described and investigated by anthropologists under the heading 'religion'. I suspect it does not. This, however, is not an alarming obstacle. For obvious historical reasons the question of the truth-claims or of the cognitive value of beliefs normally called religious has been discussed mainly within the tradition of the great universal religions which produced not only myths and rites but instruments of intellectual self-defence as well. Christianity, being by far the richest repository of endeavours to translate faith into metaphysical constructions which might be approached by means of 'natural light', provides philosophers with most of the material for their speculations. Thus what Anglo-Saxon tradition calls philosophy of religion covers roughly the same area which has been known since the Middle Ages as natural theology, meaning the rational examination of theological questions without reference to the authority of revelation. Whether such an investigation is possible at all and, if so, to what extent, was itself a matter of unceasing debate among both Christian and non-Christian thinkers, the range of viewpoints extending from those who peremptorily rejected any use of natural reason *in divinis* to those claiming that most of the essential Christian beliefs could be justified on rational grounds; certain aspects of these never-ending squabbles will have to be mentioned. It might be noted at the very outset, though, that in the description just suggested – socially established worship of the eternal reality – the concept of a 'rational religion' (not unlike that of a 'private religion') may be used only in a derivative and, strictly speaking, improper sense; there is no such thing as rational worship, *cultus rationalis*, though the concept is of Christian origin.

Inquiry into the truth-claims of religious beliefs makes up only a small part of the general examination of their cognitive function. Logically it is perfectly consistent to state that these beliefs have not a grain of truth and that an important, or indeed the chief social role of religion, is to satisfy cognitive needs. Early anthropological investigations were largely carried out on such assumptions. Religious myths were thought above all to convey a kind of knowledge, either by explaining incomprehensible natural phenomena and thereby eking out savage man's meagre stock of rational learning with arbitrary fantasies, or by providing him with distorted information on tribal history. This interpretation of myths as the pseudo-science of primitive people, as a false explanation of nature, was usually associated with the analagous interpretation of magic as a pseudo-technique, an effort to make up for poor practical skills with an imaginary technology. This approach, which goes back to antiquity, was popular among anti-religious philosophers of the Enlightenment and largely survived as a background to anthropological research, including Frazer's work, throughout the nineteenth century. A rival interpretation, going back to the Epicureans, stressed the emotional, rather than cognitive, function of myths: the fear of death and suffering, the desire to preserve a beneficial order in the chaos of the world, were supposed to supply us with an explanatory framework for the history of religions. The intellectualist approach was largely abandoned in the twentieth century in favour of various theories (Durkheim, Malinowski) which insisted on the social rather than the cognitive value of myths, on their role in integrating the society, in organizing and controlling collective emotions, in supporting the familial structure and other articulations of social life. The last decades, however, have seen a return to the intellectualist approach in an entirely new version, chiefly as a result of the work of Lévi-Strauss and his followers. The interpretation of myths in terms of their cognitive function turns out once again to be the most fruitful, according to this theory; yet not in the Enlightenment sense. The new school's effort has consisted in taking to pieces the mythological material and rearranging it in a new meaningful order, whereupon a hidden structure is revealed, one not perceived consciously by the believers but in fact providing them with intellectual tools which they use in classifying and explaining both natural and social relationships.

It is not my intention to discuss these general issues except for one remark of an epistemological, rather than an anthropological kind. All functional approaches to the investigation of myths – in terms of their social, cognitive or emotional values – have arguably a common epistemological foundation. They all imply, if they do not explicitly assume, that the language of myth is translatable into a 'normal' language – which means, into one which is understandable within the semantic rules the researcher himself is employing. The various conceptual frameworks of anthropological inquiry work, so to speak, as codes or as dictionaries which are used to transpose the ready-made mythological material into a language which is accessible and clear to contemporary minds. These codes help to disclose the hidden, 'profane' sense of mythical tales and although they do not assume that any one component of a mythological construction, however elementary, has its equivalent in the modern vocabulary – usually only larger units or even complete 'systems' are so translated – they do carry two important presuppositions. First, it is assumed that myths, as they are explicitly told and believed, have a latent meaning behind the ostensible one and that this meaning not only is not in fact perceived by those sharing a given creed, but that of necessity it cannot be perceived. Secondly, it is implied that this latent meaning, which is accessible only to the outsider-anthropologist, is the meaning *par excellence*, whereas the ostensible one, i.e., the myth as it is understood by the believers, has the function of concealing the former; this ostensible meaning appears then as a product of inescapable self-deception, of an ideological mystification or simply of ignorance.

These two premises are philosophical rather than anthropological in kind. However ingeniously developed and however efficient in intellectually organizing the mythological material, they cannot possibly be suggested by, let alone inferred from, the empirical material of an anthropologist. We need more than this material to assert that when people speak of God or of gods, of invisible forces purposely operating behind empirical events, of the sacred qualities of things, they are *in fact*, and without knowing it, speaking of something entirely different: that they express thereby social conflicts, or sexual inhibitions, or that they seek to produce a system for codifying natural phenomena, etc.

Nobody would deny that in fact people creating their myths say of themselves more than they intend to. This is true of all human products, whether material or spiritual. Yet from this common-sense generality we may not conclude that what can be discovered behind religious beliefs – their unquestionable usefulness in various 'secular' areas of life – makes up their genuine meaning. The latter assertion is arbitrary and not empirical.

The questions I am going to examine will be discussed on the shallow assumption that what people mean in religious discourse is what they ostensibly mean. This assumption is normally made not only by believers but by rationalist critics of religion as well.

This does not imply that I expect any conclusive results, positive or negative, from philosophical discussion about religious matters. I rather tend to accept the law of the infinite cornucopia which applies not only to philosophy but to all general theories in the human and social sciences: it states that there is never a shortage of arguments to support any doctrine you want to believe in for whatever reasons. These arguments, however, are not entirely barren. They have helped in elucidating the *status quaestionis* and in explaining why these questions matter, and this is what I am concerned with here. As well as giving a cursory account of various arguments which have seemed to me the most important in the ever-continuing history of the debate, I shall be trying to show how the 'rationalizers' of religious beliefs and their adversaries have forced each other to draw ultimate conclusions from their respective premises and thus how both have helped bring to light the dilemma which the sub-title of my essay hints at.

If One is not, then nothing is.

Plato, tr. B. Jowett

CHAPTER 1

God of Failures: theodicy

Apart from all the puzzles which assail us as soon as we try to understand properly God's attributes of omnipotence and of infinite goodness, it has always appeared to critics that these attributes are irreconcilable with the evil of the world. The history of the debate goes back at least to the Epicureans, and even though countless works have been written on the subject – it is hard to find a theologian or a Christian philosopher who has not tried to cope with this alarming question – the basic arguments on both sides do not seem to have changed much since St Augustine. And neither side is, nor is ever likely to be, satisfied with the arguments of the other, which has in any case been the fate of all the fundamental questions of philosophy for the last twenty-five centuries.

The Epicureans argue simply that since the world is full of evil, then God is either evil or impotent or both. An almighty, omniscient and infinitely benevolent God, assuming that such a being is logically conceivable, would have been both capable of creating a world without evil and willing to do so.

The basic counter-arguments were perhaps most clearly developed by Leibniz, who, in his *Theodicée* and in numerous other writings, time and again broached the unpleasant topic. They proceed from God to the creatures, and not the other way round, and they boil down to this.

Since God is in fact infinitely wise, good and powerful, He must have produced the best among all possible words, i.e., a world where the global amount of good outweighs the mass of evil to the maximum possible. Thus it is certain in advance, and included in the very concept of the perfect Being, that we live in the best world logically conceivable.

A sceptic who might argue that you do not need to live in this world for more than a day or two to acquire considerable doubts about its being the best universe imaginable cannot shake Leibniz's confidence. He does not deny the fact of evil, he is only certain that any other possible world would be worse than this one. He seemed to be of the opinion that this theory was a fairly optimistic one.

Leibniz's point is that some sets of things and of qualities are compatible with each other, some are not, and that this is a logical incompatibility. In other words, any possible world is offered as a package deal and God had to find out which combination of logically compatible qualities would yield the optimum good. Instead of free human subjects God could have produced creatures who were incapable of sinning but only at the price of depriving them of their free will, which inevitably includes both the possibility of sin and actual acts of sinning. And He computed that a world inhabited by sinless automata would produce significantly less good than one containing human beings who have freedom of choice and therefore might often prefer evil. God had to solve, as it were, a fairly complicated differential equation (in fact an infinite equation) to calculate in which among all possible worlds the amount of evil would be smallest compared to the amount of good; and that is the world we live in.

Leibniz does not pretend to be able to reproduce this divine computation. Only a tiny part of the existing universe, to say nothing of all the possible ones, is accessible to our minds, whereas a perfect knowledge of the whole is necessary to comprehend both the actual and the conceivable relationships between good and evil. Since neither Leibniz nor anybody else may make claims to such knowledge, we have to be satisfied with the certitude we gain from the very concept of the divine being; the necessary existence of God is proved on other grounds.

That God must have made a choice between possible worlds none of which was absolutely perfect (in the sense of being absolutely free of evil and suffering) does not suggest any limitations in Him. God cannot do what is logically impossible, but this fact imposes no boundaries on His omnipotence. He cannot do or invent absurdities; He cannot find a number exactly expressing the square root of two because this is an impossibility entailed in the very nature of mathematical objects. He could not have created a world in which the good arising from people's freedom of choice was combined with their inability to do evil, since such a world is logically as little possible as a square triangle.

Some theologians and philosophers were less convinced than Leibniz and Thomas Aquinas that to conceive of God as incapable of doing what is logically impossible did not impose on Him any limitations. Several later nominalists argued that not only physical but logical, mathematical and ethical rules had been established by God's free decisions, whose reasons are unknown to us, and that these decisions could have been different from what they were; omnipotence, they believed, is not 'omnipotence to a certain degree', such a concept being in fact nonsensical. God simply decreed that two contradictory assertions could not both be true, that two and two were four and that fornication was bad. But He could have decided otherwise and if He had done so, the principle of contradiction, the truths of mathematics and moral norms would have been opposite to what they actually are. We cannot imagine such a world, to be sure, but we may not assert, for no better reason than the poverty of our minds, that this was impossible to God; we must not measure His power by the standards of our finite, frail intelligence.

Once we accept the terrifying idea that God might have abrogated, had He so wished, the rules of logic and the moral commandments as we know them, we may, so it seems, dismiss all questions of theodicy as wrongly shaped. It might appear that the opposite is the case, that this kind of 'decretalism' (or 'theonomic positivism', as the theory under scrutiny used sometimes to be labelled) strengthens the case of those who accuse God of injustice: since nothing is impossible to Him, He *was* able to produce a world combining seemingly incompatible qualities and to give us freedom of choice within a universe without sin and without suffering. In fact, if all the rules of logic and of morality were established by an arbitrary decree of divine will and contain no intrinsic truth, there is no reason to suppose that God is bound by His rules. In other words, His goodness and wisdom need have nothing to do with what we think of as goodness and wisdom in our world as He constructed it. What seems to us incompatible may be compatible in His mind, what appears evil to us may have no recognizable sense of evil for Him. Strictly speaking, God's existence becomes irrelevant to our moral and intellectual life; He just happened to issue such and not other decrees, but they are contingent in terms of His wisdom and goodness. They might have been different. Once we know what they are – and we can know them as natural facts – their ultimate source is of no practical consequence. They are, so to speak, paradoxical entities, at once factual and necessary: factual, because we simply find them ready-made and know that they might have been different, and yet necessary, because once we know them, we cannot escape their legislative power. Thus, they are necessary only in the sense that applies to general empirical truths: gold is heavier than water, but there are no compelling logical reasons why this relationship could not be reversed; nevertheless, we know that it is always so and in this, and only this, sense is the relationship necessary.

God is He for Whose will no cause or ground may be laid
down as its rule and standard; for nothing is on a level with
it or above it, but it is itself the rule for all things. If any
rule or standard, or cause or ground, existed for it, it
could no longer be the will of God. What God wills is not
right because He ought, or was bound, so to will; on the
contrary, what takes place must be right, because He so
wills it. Causes and grounds are laid down for the will of
the creature, but not for the will of the Creator – unless
you set another Creator over Him!

Martin Luther, tr. J. I. Packer and A. R. Johnston

And indeed, the theory which made logical, mathematical, and moral laws dependent entirely on God's free and
arbitrary decree was, historically speaking, an important
step in getting rid of God altogether. God's essence and
existence were divorced in such a way that He has become
in fact, though not in doctrine, a *deus otiosus* who,
having issued his laws, then abandoned the world. In the
history of ideas the nominalist tendency to devolve the
responsibility for our logic and ethics on the Creator's
arbitrary fiat marked the beginning of His separation from
the universe. If there is no way in which the actual fiat can
be understood in terms of God's essence, there is simply
no way from creatures to God. Consequently it does not
matter much, in our thinking and actions, whether He
exists at all.

Confusion on this issue was inevitable, as the nominalist
doctrine seemed to make the world more, and not less,
dependent on God and to enhance, rather than to limit, His
omnipotence. The confusion is particularly striking in the
history of Descartes' legacy. Christian critics pointed out
that Cartesian metaphysics had in fact relegated God to the
position of an indifferent creator (Pascal's famous *chique-*

naude: Descartes would have liked to do without God altogether; eventually he permitted God to give the world a flip, after which he had no further need of Him). Descartes' defenders replied that his doctrine, far from enfeebling God's royal rights and limiting His power, extended them by making even the apparently obvious axioms of mathematics dependent on divine will. Ostensibly this was so; yet the results turned against the premises. There is no doubt about Descartes' genuine belief in God and Providence; still, Pascal was right. Descartes barred the road from Nature to God by breaking the link between God's essence and His actual legislation; he was thereby, in spite of his intentions, to become a forerunner of deists.

The separation of God's will from His essence meant His separation from the creatures. And it implied, in fact, that

---

In saying, therefore, that things are not good according to any standard of goodness, but simply by the will of God, it seems to me that one destroys, without realizing it, all the love of God and all his glory; for why praise him for what he has done, if he would be equally praiseworthy in doing the contrary? Where will be his justice and his wisdom if he has only a certain despotic power, if arbitrary will takes the place of reasonableness, and if in accord with the definition of tyrants, justice consists in that which is pleasing to the most powerful?

Leibniz, tr. A. R. Chandler

God's acts are free in the same sense as ours (or at least as we usually imagine them), in other words that God enjoys the freedom of *indifferentia*. The argument sometimes advanced to defend this concept was that if we deny God freedom of decision in that sense, we suggest that He is compelled to act in a particular way because there are norms – logical or moral – which He is bound to obey and over which

He has no power; He simply cannot – so the argument goes – devise a world in which killing one's father would be morally commendable, because killing one's father is intrinsically evil, whatever God might wish; and likewise He cannot cancel the validity of the rules of the syllogism, however strongly He might dislike them.

Thomas Aquinas' and Leibniz's notion of God's freedom did not imply, of course, anything which suggested that God was subjected to rules He himself had found, as it were, ready-made, so that He stood helplessly under a foreign jurisdiction. The absolute Being, as they thought of Him, had no attributes and carried out no acts which might have been different from His essence. If we speak of God's qualities and works as conceptually separable objects, that is only because this is the way in which a finite intelligence tries to grasp the Infinity it cannot properly understand. In God Himself essence and existence converge and this implies that His will is identical with His essence. God neither obeys rules which are valid regardless of His will nor produces these rules according to His whims or as the result of deliberating various options; He *is* those rules. Unlike humans, God never faces alternative possibilities and then freely decides which of them He ought to choose; His decisions are necessary aspects of his Being (provision being made, again, for the improper use of the word 'aspects', given the absolute unity of the Divine) and therefore they could not have been different from what they are; yet they are free in the sense that no superior powers, no norms of validity independent of God, bind Him. He *is* what He does, decides, orders. Consequently, we may say neither that the definitions of what is good or true *precede* God so that He is under an obligation to bow before them, nor that He precedes them and calls them out of nothing into existence by an act of royal edict or by pulling them from His magic hat. There is no relation of precedence in God: neither in a temporal sense, as there is no time in God, nor logically, as logical precedence cannot be properly applied to the unspeakable unity.

... We must say that the power of God has a limit and we must not, under pretext of honouring God, annul this limitation. For if the power of God were infinite, it would follow inevitably that it would not know itself; for the infinite is by nature incomprehensible.

Origen, tr. H. Bettenson

And thus Plato's tormenting question in the *Eutyphron* – is what is holy loved by the gods because it is holy, or is it holy because it is loved by the gods? – turns out to be wrongly put if we consider God's perfect self-identity and indivisibility. It is not the case that God first loved what is good because it is good irrespective of His decisions, and it is not the case that He has proclaimed something to be good, and – since, but not before – His statement acquires the force of law. Such formulations of the question wrongly imply that relationships like 'before' or 'after' might be reasonably employed when the absolute Being is spoken of.

It was not only Christian writers who stressed this point. So did Spinoza, when he affirmed that God is perfectly free in the sense that no cause other than Himself prompts Him to act and that all His actions are necessary since they follow His immutable nature. According to Spinoza – and this seems to be a fair account, even though he does not explicitly say so – to deny the necessity of God's actions would amount to conceiving of Him as a being who at a certain stage is not determined to do something and then at the next stage determines Himself or takes a decision; this image of God would be both false and blasphemous, as it would imply that a distinction may be drawn in Him between *potentia* and *actus*, between what He can be and what He in fact is, such a distinction being by definition inconceivable given the pure actuality of the divine existence.

Almost all of Spinoza's Christian critics, both his contemporaries (like Lambert van Velthuysen) and later commentators (like Jacobi) condemned this doctrine of God's necessity as essentially anti-Christian. It is, however, by no means certain that it is so. On the assumption that God is not the demiurge of the Platonists but that He is the absolute being – as He has been in the Christian tradition since the second century AD and in Thomist metaphysics in particular – it is not clear how the quality of freedom, except as Spinoza defines it (i.e., the condition of not being subjected to any extraneous cause), can be attributed to Him. He cannot be free in the sense of ever being in a state of indecision, of deliberating about His choice, of having in himself potentialities which will never be or have never been actuated. In short, He cannot be free in the sense that human creatures are; it makes no sense to say that He could have done something He did not, since He is everything He can be. Spinoza's concept is no doubt incompatible with the Christian tradition. It deprives God of a number of qualities which are necessary to being a recognizable *person*: He does not love particular men, He has no mercy, and extension is His attribute. Yet, by describing His actions as necessary Spinoza did not manifestly depart from Christian metaphysics; indeed he wanted to be as faithful as possible to the notion of pure actuality.

He may, however, have gone further than he intended. He posed, even if not explicitly, two formidable questions which Christian metaphysics, indeed any metaphysics of one God, cannot escape.

First, if the absolute may be called free only in the sense that nothing other than Himself causes His acts, and necessary in the sense that no potentialities can be concealed in Him, that He is whatever He can be, then it would be proper to say that both these attributes – freedom and necessity – lose their meaning when applied to Him. Our freedom, as we conceive of it, implies that we are not totally free, or that our actions are limited by many circumstances over which we have no power; we are capable of thinking of our freedom only against the background of our non-freedom; the reason we can think that we are free is because we know what it means to be unfree and vice versa. Neither of these two concepts could have emerged or could have been understood without the other. Since God's acts are both free and necessary in a sense that ours cannot be and since both qualities in Him follow from His being *actus purus* (which implies that He cannot be free in the sense of bringing potentialities into reality and cannot be necessary in the sense of being subject to limitations 'from outside'), it appears that it is the same thing to say that His actions are free and that they are necessary. This amounts to saying that the absolute Being is beyond the opposition free/necessary and thus that we cannot understand Him.

Secondly, if neither freedom nor limitation nor compulsion as we understand those words can be predicated of Him, He is suspected of not being a person in the sense that each of us is. That I am a person implies that I am both free and limited: free, as the conscious author of certain of my actions which I may or may not perform; and limited, insofar as I am aware of other persons and things as alien, as something I am not. God is neither: there are no actions He can perform and does not, and He perceives no persons or things as belonging to an alien world; in keeping with the very concept of pure actuality and of infinity, He perceives everything, as it were, from within and therefore He *is* everything (*Deus est quodammodo omnia*, as St Thomas has it), since to perceive a thing 'from outside' means to be limited by it.

Again, if God is free and if He is a person, this has to be in a sense we are radically unable to comprehend; as applied to Him, such notions have a meaning infinitely remote from their normal usage. To say that they are used and are made

... Being is God. This proposition is obvious, in the first place, because if being is something different from God, God does not exist and there is no God. For how can he exist, or how can anything exist, if there is another existence foreign and distinct from being? ... Beyond being and before being there is nothing. Therefore, if being is other than God or foreign to God, God would be nothing.

Meister Eckhard, tr. R. B. Blakney

intelligible by analogy to the qualities that we humans possess does not help much: there can be no analogy between the finite and the absolute, no conceptual projection from limited beings to infinitude. In other words, there is no way of grasping God conceptually except by means which are not only imperfect but positively distorting because they reduce God to a finite demiurge.

This is not the end of the story, though. Before carrying it further I have to go back to the most classic of all the classic dilemmas of theology: omnipotence and evil.

Let us stick, for the sake of argument, to the God of Thomas Aquinas and Leibniz, who, without being in any way limited, cannot do what is logically impossible or morally wrong because the corresponding rules are identical with Himself. This argument may be restated, somewhat frivolously, by saying that the very concept of the absolute Being implies that He cannot commit suicide, which is what He would be doing if He abrogated rules identical with Himself; the inability of the absolute Being to commit suicide does not impose any limits upon His omnipotence (and to limit omnipotence means to annihilate it); His existence being necessary – whether or not we can intellectually comprehend this kind of necessity – the idea of God's self-destruction is self-contradictory or analytically impossible.

Thus there is only one true God and only one cause which is
the true cause; and one must not imagine that something
which precedes an effect is its real cause. Even God cannot
– according to the light of Reason – give His power to the
creatures, He cannot make them true causes, He cannot
make them gods . . . Bodies, spirits, pure intelligences, all
these are unable to do anything . . . He moves our hand
even when we use it against His orders; for He complains
through His prophet (Isai. 13:24) that we let Him serve
our unjust and criminal wishes.

Nicholas Malebranche

Therefore, when we say that God cannot, for instance,
abolish the rules of logic or of ethics, the word 'cannot', like
all the other words we employ to picture Him, has a meaning
different from its common usage ('I cannot lift this stone', 'I
cannot speak Japanese', etc.). Far from referring to a
person's contingent inability to perform an action, it
signifies God's plenitude of being. Since the only act God
'cannot' carry out is to kill Himself and since this inability is
included in His necessary existence which in its turn implies
the absence of any limitations, it appears that when saying
He 'cannot' do something, we simply reaffirm His omnipotence; He 'cannot' stop being almighty. This, I trust, is a fair
account of the notion of the Absolute in the major currents
of the Christian and neo-platonist traditions.

This notion does not suggest that God, although the
quality of 'being free' may not be attributed to Him in the
same way it may be to us, could not have endowed some of
His creatures with freedom as we understand it nor does it
imply that such freedom was bound to be on balance more
beneficial – whatever this means – than its absence,
assuming, as all the authors of theodicies do, that freedom is
necessarily coupled with evil and that being free is logically
incompatible with being unable to do evil.

This last point was sometimes contested on the ground that God might have produced creatures who were free, and thus capable of doing evil, and yet who were constructed in such a way that they would never realize this ability by committing evil acts; there is, so the argument runs, no logical incompatibility between being able to do evil and not actually doing it. If so, then the basis of theodicy seems to crumble. The counter-argument (used by Plantinga) maintains that it is hard to see what difference there is between a mankind none of whose members would be free to do evil and another consisting of creatures who are free to do evil yet never actually do it because they are so programmed by their maker. There is nothing logically incompatible in the idea of

---

It is better that God had ordained sin than that he had prevented it, which he could not have done without having forced and driven man like a stone or a block. But then his name would not be recognized and praised by men. The reason: they would have presumed, since they would be aware of no sin, that they were just as righteous as God. Therefore it is infinitely better to have ordained than to have prevented sin. For sin is over against God to be reckoned as nothing; and however great it might be, God can, will, and indeed already has, overcome it for himself to his own eternal praise, without harm for any creatures. But God would not have been able to alter his own regulations, to maintain his creatures without sin, without disadvantage to his eternally abiding truth. For he could never with full praise have been praised, which was the first and only reason for having begun to create.

Hans Denck (1526) tr. G. H. Williams

---

a person who, while being free to perform evil acts, refrains from actually performing them, but there is no recognizable difference between all people being unable to do evil and all people being able to do it, yet so constructed that they never in fact do it. It appears that for all practical, and indeed all theoretical purposes, such creatures would be unfree to do evil and therefore unfree *tout court.*

On the other hand, in strictly Christian terms, this counter-argument does not sound quite convincing; it might be pointed out that Christians believe that there *is* a realm in which rational creatures are both free and in a sense – not quite comprehensible to us – incapable of doing evil; this is the case of all the denizens of heaven and of faithful angels as well.

Still, even if theodicy may be cleared of inconsistency on this particular point, that does not make it immune to other objections.

Let us assume, in accordance with the arguments of Leibniz and in fact of all Christian apologists, that human freedom inevitably breeds evil and suffering. It is indeed plausible to argue that a perfect world, combining human creativity with a conflict-free order, is inconceivable; by the sheer fact of being creative and unpredictable, people have to have conflicting desires and incompatible aims. To admit that is not to vindicate a theodicy, of course. How do we know that, as the result of a computation performed by God, the global amount of good in such a world is incomparably larger than in any imaginary world of sinless mechanisms? It is obvious that we cannot derive this knowledge from any empirical investigation: not only could we never finish the calculation which implies a complete account of all possible facts and relationships in all real and possible worlds, but we could not even start our work since we lack any conceptual instruments for measuring the relative amounts of good and evil; there is no means of reducing the infinite variety of moral and physical evil to homogeneous quantifiable units. Therefore the faith that the universe generates the minimum amount of evil or that ultimately 'whatever is, is right' can be founded only on trust in God (which is what the Christian word 'faith' originally means). Without this act of trust any speculative theodicy is futile. From the belief in a God who is both omnipotent (in the sense just discussed) and good the relative perfection of the world may be deduced; however, since God's goodness cannot be known from collecting empirical evidence (even on the assumption that there are logically admissible ways to demonstrate His existence and omnipotence), faith in the sense of 'trust' has to precede any reasoning. Yet trust cannot form a link in logical procedure. It is an act of moral, not intellectual, commitment. Thus, if theodicy is possible at all, it cannot be a positive proof of any theory concerning perfection or the balance of good and evil in the actual world. It might only be, if successful, a proof that a world with as much evil as ours and both created and ruled by a benevolent and almighty providence is not an inherently impossible or self-contradictory entity. And it would imply that in any case we can never know *how* it is not self-contradictory.

Now it is necessary that what comes after the First should exist, and therefore that the Last should exist; and this is matter, which possesses nothing at all of the Good. And in this way too evil is necessary.

Plotinus, tr. A. H. Armstrong

This seems to have been the genuine task of theodicy, for that matter. Yet people who want to be convinced that their life is cared for by a good warden, all the monstrosities of the world notwithstanding, are not willing to be satisfied with this meagre result. They desperately seek a positive certainty that their life *is* in fact protected by the divine wisdom, that the world has a hidden meaning which is bound to be revealed, on earth or in heaven, and that human destiny, both individual and universal, will turn out to be a history of victorious justice. This need a speculative theodicy can by no means satisfy; still less can its other version which tries to prove that evil is a necessary component of the splendid harmony of the whole of the universe, that whatever seems to us meaningless corruption, aimless destruction, diabolic viciousness, unredeemable torment, all the absurdity and horror of life, when seen from the vantage point of divine reason turn out to be so many contributions to universal salvation and final glory. This attempt to reconcile God's wisdom with human misery is especially characteristic of all those currents within Christianity which – from Erigena to Teilhard de Chardin – succumbed to the temptation of pantheistic belief in the total absorption, at the end of time, of whatever the history of the world has produced. From this standpoint evil is ultimately not evil at all: we only think of it as such because the complete history of salvation is beyond our reach, because we absolutize certain fragments of it without realizing that in the divine plan they serve the cause of good. Thus the question of evil is not so much solved as cancelled, since all the things we imagine to be evil are merely bricks for building a future perfection, and nothing is going to be wasted in the process.

Apart from its potentially dangerous corollaries (it seems that whatever I do I contribute willy-nilly to the implementation of God's benevolent redemption-blueprint; thus I do not need to worry much about the rightness of my conduct) this doctrine is very poorly designed if it is to appease the hunger of people searching for meaning in their misery. To those in despair and agony it is no consolation, indeed it might sound outrageous, to be told that there is nothing wrong with their suffering once it is seen as an involuntary contribution to the beauty of the universe, or that the wickedness of those who cause them to suffer is good insofar as it makes the splendour of the Whole shine brighter.

And yet the problem of theodicy, far from being invented for the amusement of speculative minds, has strong and unwithering roots in the everyday experience of those who refuse to admit that suffering and evil are just suffering and evil, plain facts meaning nothing, related to nothing, justified by nothing. Empirically considered, this seems obviously the case: no rational inquiry into the origin of evil can reveal more than facts causing other facts, whose succession is governed by natural regularities and countless hazards; no sense, no redemption, no remuneration; our world having once emerged for no purpose, nobody knows exactly how, it follows its course perfectly indifferent to our wishes and it will certainly end one way or another: the earth incinerated by the dying sun, the universe immobilized forever in thermodynamic equilibrium, the solar system reduced to a black hole. As to human destiny, 'they were born, they suffered, they died', as Anatole France's shortest world history would have it. Ultimately the history of the universe appears to be the history of the defeat of Being by Nothingness: matter, life, the human race, human intelligence and creativity – everything is bound to end in defeat; all our efforts, suffering and delights will perish forever in the void, leaving no traces behind.

This sounds banal and it is banal and therefore important, as the banal is no less than what is known and experienced by all. It is by no means the case that the fear of ultimate defeat is a contrivance of modern existential ontology or an effect of the recent shadow of global all-destructive war. It is to be found in many great documents of ancient faith: in *The Epic of Gilgamesh*, in *Rig Veda*, in the *Bhagavad Gita*, in the book of Job, in the Gospels, in the Edda and in many recorded myths of archaic religions, among peoples with a rather scanty knowledge of the laws of thermodynamics and of modern astrophysics; yet they knew death, pain, separation, cruelty, wickedness, treason, vain efforts and frustrated desires, and there is no reason to think that they experienced these in any other way than we do. They knew evil and defeat and coped with them. In various forms they affirmed their belief that throughout all the changes another permanent reality persists: immune to corruption, thus inaccessible to our eyes and ears, and yet not entirely beyond experience, it is a place where everything we do and everything that occurs in the world is somehow eternally

---

Now this, brethren, is the Ariyan Truth about *Suffering*: Birth is Suffering, Decay is Suffering, Sickness is Suffering, Death is Suffering, likewise Sorrow and Grief, Woe, Lamentation and Despair. To be conjoined with things we dislike, to be separated from things we like – that also is Suffering. Not to get what one wants – that also is Suffering. In a word, this Body, this five-fold mass which is based on *Grasping*, that is Suffering.

Now this, brethren, is the Ariyan Truth about *the Origin of Suffering*: It is that Craving that leads downwards to birth, along with the Lure and Lust that lingers longingly now here, now there: namely, the Craving for Sensation, the Craving to be born again, the Craving to have done with rebirth. Such, brethren, is the Ariyan Truth about *the Origin of Suffering*.

And this, brethren, is the Ariyan Truth about *the Ceasing of Suffering*: Verily it is utter passionless cessation of the giving up, the forsaking, the release from, the absence of longing for, this *Craving*.

Attributed to Buddha, tr. F. L. Woodward

---

preserved; therefore our achievements and pains are not in vain, after all; through them reality grows and enriches itself, as it were; they are not engulfed and annihilated in the abyss of time but are captured in the never perishing abode of Being; and only in eternal (i.e., timeless, not everlasting) reality can Nothingness be defeated.

Nothing could be easier, indeed, than Voltaire's sneering at Leibniz and Pope, as nothing seems more absurd than to repeat 'whatever is, is right' in the face of all the misfortunes that befall us. Yet everyday experience shows unmistakably

---

In the beginning all was Brahman, One and infinite. He is beyond north and south, and east and west, and beyond what is above and below; His infinity is everywhere. In him there is neither east nor west.

The spirit supreme is immeasurable, inapprehensible, beyond conception, never born, beyond reasoning, beyond thought. His vastness is the vastness of space.

At the end of the worlds, all things sleep: he alone is awake in eternity. Then from his infinite space new worlds rise and awake, a universe which is a vastness of thought. In the consciousness of Brahman the universe is, and into it returns.

From: Maitri Upanishad, *tr. Juan Mascaró*

---

that people who are able to absorb their misery, thanks to their strong belief in a purposeful order wherein everything is ultimately given a meaning, are better prepared to sustain the inevitable blows of destiny and not to succumb to despair; the testimonies of those who survived the protracted horrors of concentration camps seem to confirm the common-sense expectation that such people would do better in morally resisting unbearable pressures and thus increasing their physical chances of survival. Needless to say, no such facts 'prove' that the actual content of those beliefs is true in the normal sense of the word; the point is only that, in the face of such trivial observations, the standard rationalist rejoinder, 'a religious world view can act as a source of consolation', turns against Voltaire, rather than against Pangloss. The latter probably would not have outlived his ordeal had he not stuck firmly to his faith in providential wisdom, and so as a technique for survival his creed was vindicated and not absurd at all.

If it is the case that belief in the ultimate and beneficial meaning of whatever happens is useful as a homeostatic mechanism helping people to adjust to, and to live through, the various stresses of life, this nevertheless seems logically irrelevant to the question of the truth-claims of such a belief; at first glance these claims are neither reinforced nor weakened. In fact both the believers and the foes of religion often appeal to the utility of belief (and to other profane functions of a religious world view as well: moral, social, cognitive) in promoting their respective causes. The former tend to stress that trust in Providence, precisely because it benefits our living, is 'natural'; consequently a religious world perception is as much a part of our natural endowment as our having two eyes rather than three. This involved, it would seem, the old belief according to which Nature does nothing in vain and could not possibly have implanted in us desires which cannot in principle be satisfied. The enemies of religion stress that, on the contrary, the fictitious character of religious beliefs is revealed by the compensatory function they do or might perform as psychological defence mechanisms; if an illusion is useful, this does not make it any less an illusion. On the contrary, once we are able to understand the psychological processes which induce people to accept certain beliefs, it appears quite natural to think that we have a perfectly sufficient basis for dismissing their truth-claims. Clearly, however, the fact that we know of 'irrational' causes for a belief does not lead logically to the conclusion that the belief is false. But the very fact that people have strong motives for accepting a belief makes the other evidence they provide in its support seem *prima facie* suspect or at any rate less, rather than more, credible.

The epistemological status of the question is perhaps more complicated than the arguments above might have suggested and I will return to it later on, after having discussed other sides of the notion of truth when applied to

---

The weak and ill-constituted shall perish: first principle of *our* philanthropy. And one shall help them to do so. What is more harmful than any vice? Active sympathy for the ill-constituted and weak – Christianity . . .

Christianity is called the religion of pity. Pity stands in antithesis to the tonic emotions which enhance the energy of the feeling of life: it has a depressive effect. One loses force when one pities . . . Pity on the whole thwarts the law of evolution, which is the law of *selection*.

Friedrich Nietzsche, tr. R. J. Hollingdale

---

the specific area of worship. For now, it need be stressed only that a religious world perception is indeed able to teach us *how to be a failure*. And the latent assumption behind such teaching is that on earth everybody *is* a failure. This is an integral element in both Christian and Buddhist tradition. Both lead us to perceive that all happiness and all enjoyment in our short journey through matter are so many self-delusions and that if we are happy, this is only *mala fide*. Here Buddhist wisdom goes further and perhaps is more consistent than Christianity. The Christian message, to be sure, has never included a promise of temporal happiness; it has never let us expect that the disciples of Christ would enjoy both the delights of earthly life and the blessedness of union with God. It rather emphasized the misery of our bodily existence as a normal precondition of beatitude in the heavenly kingdom. Had it promised to the faithful both kinds of reward, terrestrial and celestial, who could resist? It taught that more often than not the wicked would be victorious and the virtuous persecuted in this vale of tears. Nothing is easier than to scoff at this doctrine, to quote all the examples from the history of the *Ecclesia triumphans* and to show how frequently the idea of the incurable misery of life has been used for inglorious purposes. Still, its basic insight – that happiness is an escape from reality – runs through the entire history of philosophy and religion and has not only metaphysical but psychological authenticity.

But from the utter fading out and ending of Ignorance comes also the ending of Actions: from the ending of Actions comes the ending of Consciousness: from the ending of Consciousness comes the ending of Name-and-Shape: from the ending of Name-and-Shape comes the ending of Sense: from the ending of Sense comes the ending of Contact: from the ending of Contact comes the ending of Feeling: from the ending of Feeling comes the ending of Craving: from the ending of Craving comes the ending of Grasping: from the ending of Grasping comes the ending of Becoming: from the ending of Becoming comes the ending of Birth: from the ending of Birth comes the ending of Age-and-death, Sorrow and Grief, Woe, Lamentation, and Despair. Such is the ending of all this mass of Ill.

Attributed to Buddha, tr. F. L. Woodward

Yet Buddha's teaching did not stop at the opposition of material to spiritual life. It is not simply our corruptible body which makes us suffer, it is the very fact that each of us tries to assert and to enhance his own separate and illusory existence. In order to be free from evil it is not enough to be free from the bondage of the body; one has to get rid of all desires which maintain our self-imposed isolation and this means discarding all desires altogether. If, instead of employing our intelligence in satisfying our needs – a vain effort anyway, since the mounting spiral of needs never stops – we try to suppress them and to realize that both the world and the self are illusion, we can achieve a state of plenitude wherein no imaginary beings imprison us in our apparent exclusivity and separateness from the divine.

I am not competent to join the never-ending and centuries-old discussion about how this absolute state (admittedly inexpressible in the tongue of mortals) is or is not compatible with the continuation of our present conscious life as we know it, in what sense nirvana equals 'extinction' and to what extent it does or does not correspond to the *unio mystica* as it has been depicted – again, in avowedly awkward terms – by Christian contemplatives. Clearly, both cases involve a strong feeling that separation from the absolute Being is the root of evil and pain and the way of return to non-separation is open. The nature of the obstacles to be razed before this stage is reached and the nature of non-separation itself are differently identified; Buddhist tradition certainly is more emphatic in seeing the main obstacle (indeed the only one, others being derivative) in our obstinate desire to assert our exclusive existence not only in moral terms, i.e., in terms of selfishness and greed, but in ontological terms as well, and this means: my sheer desire to be myself is the root of unavoidable evil. To understand one's disease is not only a precondition of healing – as in psychoanalysis – but is actually the cure, and to see properly the attachment to one's separate existence is to perceive it as in a strange sense unreal. Thus a Buddhist contemplative is capable of saying 'I do not exist' and of literally meaning it: an utterance which Christians, with some notable exceptions, would normally understand only in a metaphorical sense, in spite of the importance the theme of self-destructive love has had in the history of Western mystics. Is nirvana a state of 'happiness without a happy person', as a Polish philosopher, Henryk Elzenberg, put it? I shall revert to this topic in discussing mystical religiosity.

The Buddhist way of answering the question 'what is wrong with the world and our life in it?' identifies evil as an ontological event: it follows fatefully from the very fact of self-imposed separation, *individuatio*. The distinction between evil in the moral and in the physical sense is either treated as secondary or even goes unnoticed, whereas it is fundamental to Christian perception. One is tempted to say that in a consistent Buddhist framework the act of creation itself, by producing more than One, amounts to producing evil. Yet in Christian terms the act of creation is good by definition and produces nothing but good. Evil is nothingness, *privatio*, lack of what ought to be; whatever is, is good as far as it is (*esse et bonum convertuntur*) since *esse* is entirely from God.

Having no ontological foundation, evil is a matter of evil will (and the purely human, i.e., self-centred, will is rebellious and by definition evil). The Christian tradition has always made a distinction between *malum culpae*, moral evil, and *malum poenae*, suffering. To inflict suffering on others out of hate, anger or selfish motives is evil in a moral sense; to suffer is not, of course.

Since suffering obviously may result from natural causes, rather than from the evil will of people, it might appear that the reasons for it have to be sought elsewhere. Yet it is not so. In Christian terms suffering, whether natural or inflicted by people, is ultimately reducible to the same source: separation from God, yet a separation not ontological (i.e., implied by the very act of creation) but moral. Deliberate disobedience brought about both moral evil and the general corruption of Nature with suffering as an unavoidable result. Therefore suffering inflicted by Nature is really *malum poenae*, punishment for mankind's sins. This is a biblical view which, particularly in St Augustine, has become a part of orthodox teaching.

We touch here one of the most sensitive and most enigmatic points in Christian doctrine, one which has always been a favourite target of rationalist derision: the so-called question of collective responsibility, collective punishment, original sin and redemption. It used to be attacked on two grounds, logical and moral.

The moral argument is simple. It amounts to the commonsense observation that it runs against our normal moral assumptions to accept that God punishes innocent people for the crimes of others, or that He inflicts unspeakable torments on the entire species for millennia because of their remote ancestors' single act of disobedience, and this rather a minor one ('why, they just stole an apple!'). This may be a childish critique of a childish story bearing little resemblance to the Christian teaching; it deserves some attention, though, as it is to be found frequently in the rationalist philosophers' armoury.

The logical argument points out the vain efforts of those who, not satisfied with a general explanation of suffering as punishment, seek to trace the hand of divine justice in every particular fact; they try to discover specific reasons for their own or other people's pains and misfortunes in the identifiable offences they have committed and if they try hard enough their research is invariably successful. And so their trust in God's wisdom is always justified. The logical

---

Doth someone say that there are gods above?
There are not; no, there are not. Let no fool,
Led by the old false fable, thus deceive you.
Look at the facts themselves, yielding my words
No undue credence; for I say that kings
Kill, rob, break oath, lay cities waste by fraud,
And doing thus are happier than those
Who live calm pious lives day after day.
How many little states that serve the gods
Are subject to the godless but more strong,
Made slaves by might of a superior army.

Euripides, tr. J. A. Symonds

---

poverty of this kind of confirmation is demonstrated in the standard Popperian way. The belief which people imagine is being confirmed in the facts of life – so the argument goes – is utterly unfalsifiable and thereby powerless as an explanatory device. Given the simple fact that very few of us are either saints or absolutely corrupted, there is no moment in our life in which we do not deserve, in terms of perfect justice, to be both chastised and rewarded. The believers might fancy that whatever happens to them, fortunate or otherwise, is to be related to their virtuous or sinful deeds, and if they interpret events on those lines they do not need to fear that any fact will contradict the theory, since the theory is able to absorb all imaginable facts and is thus empirically empty. And indeed, if explanation in terms of direct penalty or remuneration seems implausible, other divine intentions can always be substituted with the same result: bad luck which I cannot relate to any of my misdeeds may be interpreted as a warning or a trial – both means of divine intervention amply documented in the Old Testament (though if I am really incapable of tracing my misfortunes to my sinful past I am naturally suspected of blindness and self-complacency, as it is *a priori* certain that I am guilty at any given moment; is it not true that '*non est qui faciat bonum, non est usque ad unum*'?). On the other hand, if an unexpected happy event occurs, with no particular merits on my part having clearly contributed to it, this may be an encouragement or just a generous smile of Providence. There are no imaginable empirical circumstances which might refute or injure my belief.

The logical critique is obviously sound, but only on condition that God is an explanatory hypothesis in the scientific sense and that His moral responses to human actions follow a regular pattern which we can both discern and use for predicting future events. To hold that view amounts simply to asserting that the world, both natural and social, is governed by moral, instead of (and not in addition to) physical and biological laws, or that the latter do not operate. Yet this has never been the teaching of Christianity; never, that is, since Jesus said that God lets the sun shine on the good and the evil and sends the rain on the just and the unjust alike. The view of the temporal world in which the mechanisms of justice are infallibly at work and all our actions are properly and quickly compensated according to moral rules is so absurdly removed from everyday experience that the human race could probably not have survived if it has ever seriously given credence to it, for in this case people would simply have ignored natural laws. Indeed in popular Christian teaching the stress has always lain on the lack or moral compensation in temporal affairs, in keeping with the common-sense view: evil is powerful, virtue is penalized and so on. This doctrine stimulated, for that matter, another frequent line of attack on Christianity in terms of its social function: the charge has been that its promise of heavenly balance imposed on people a passivity in the face of evil and injustice, deprived them of the will and ability to revolt or simply to improve their lot. This criticism, exercised by socialists in particular, has been by no means unfounded in various historical periods, even though it has largely lost its force by now.

It is true, on the other hand, that the hope of earthly recompense for our virtues (prosperity in business as a sign of grace, etc.) has not been altogether absent in the Christian, especially in the Protestant, world view. However, the essence of Christian teaching has never been to assert a magical link between our behaviour and the responses of destiny. It has rather been: 'God's ways of governing the world are incomprehensible to us, we may be certain that His justice will ultimately prevail, good and evil will be properly rewarded; this, however, has nothing to do with our earthly happiness or misfortunes.' In short, the attitude of a Christian is not to expect supernaturally produced responses to his moral conduct; it consists in trusting God. In the face of disasters produced by forces over which we have no control he is taught to 'render to God his suffering' and to be confident that the apparent absurdities of life have a hidden meaning he is unable to decode.

Everything ultimately goes back to the basic principle: trust God. We have no clues to God's ciphers. We may and ought to believe, in religious terms, that events subject to natural regularities are nevertheless the signs of His presence or, to use the traditional metaphysical idiom, that the teleological order of things does not abolish the order of 'efficient causes' but is mysteriously superimposed on them; therefore we may trust that whatever happens is both causally determined and included in a purposeful construction and thereby providentially ordained. It is not the case that the physical universe goes its own way, indifferent and aimless, and that only in the darkness of the unknown 'beyond' will a balance conforming to our wishes and moral sense be restored.

. . . Predestination is part of providence. Providence does not suppress secondary causes, but achieves its effects through subordinating their operation to itself. God provides effects in nature by ordaining natural causes to produce them, without which they would not be produced. He predestines the salvation of a man in the same way, subordinating to the ordinance of predestination everything which can help him toward salvation, whether it be his own prayers, or the prayers of another, or good works of any other kind, while his salvation would not be attained without them.

St Thomas Aquinas, tr. A. M. Fairweather

No, both orders, causal and goal-related, work together, though only the first is within the range of our eyes and hands. Yet, that it is so we can never prove in the sense that

'proof' has in empirical investigations. We have to trust
God's wisdom and benevolence; but even 'trust' has in this
context a meaning different from its usual one. Trust can
be an expectation based on probabilistic calculations or on
ordinary experience: to trust means to anticipate that an
object or a person will be as reliable as it or he used to be
(to trust one's car, to trust a debtor or a physician). In
personal contacts another sense of 'trusting' emerges; a
non-calculated confidence, an acceptance of another
person in advance, no matter whether we have ever had the
opportunity to verify her or his reliability and even if we
have reason to doubt it. This comes closer to what a
believer feels in his attitude to God. God is not reliable and
cannot be trusted on the basis of a historical record
showing that whenever His children asked for His help, it
was invariably given according to their wishes; they cannot
escape the conclusion that fortune and misery are distri-
buted at random and not in agreement with the rules of
justice as they normally understand it. They accept God's
will as it is manifested in the chaotic mass of incomprehensible accidents, of blindly operating laws of nature, of
patent injustice in human affairs. They trust God before
His wisdom and goodness are experimentally tested and
irrespective of the results of possible tests. Such results
indeed are never conclusive: occasionally they seem to be
positive, more often they defeat expectations; yet trust is
not shaken precisely because it is not based on empirical
evidence but given *a priori*. Once it is given, but not
before, believers can perceive God's hand at work in events
and they frequently have the feeling of a world being wisely
governed in spite of all the horrors that seem to defy such
an assessment. Some think that they are able to read
providential signs in all the hazards of life; some, in
moments of sudden enlightenment, grasp the latent meaning of all the vicissitudes they have endured. Again, they
cannot 'prove' it, yet they are satisfied with their reading.

One may retort that if God indeed wants to convey to us meaningful signs of His rule, His actions appear counter-productive since we are not capable of comprehending them. What is the purpose of speaking to people in a language they do not know and can never properly learn? But this is to beg the question. Whoever believes in God's presence in the world, has to admit that empirically His presence is ambiguous. Clearly, there would be no need of faith if the course of world affairs followed directly and unmistakably the norms of justice; this would mean that we live in Paradise. Adam and Eve did not believe in God's existence in the sense that their descendants were to (exception being made for Abraham, Moses and a few mystics); they lived in a real theocracy, under God's direct and visible government. Life in exile is bound to be ambiguous, God's signs are never clear, trusting Him is inevitably to defy the limits of natural knowledge.

If there was no obscurity, man would not feel his corruption, and if there was no light, man would have no hope for a remedy. Thus it is not only just, but useful to us that God is hidden in part and discovered in part, for to man it is as dangerous to know God without knowing his own misery as it is to know his misery without knowing God.

Blaise Pascal

Then the question occurs: why should we, why should anybody trust God or admit His existence at all? If 'why' means 'on what grounds similar to those we refer to in accepting scientific hypotheses?' there is no answer, as there are no grounds of this kind. But the question may be reversed: what reason can be adduced for holding that the rules normally followed in testing and in provisionally accepting scientific hypotheses define implicitly or explicitly the limits of what is meaningful or acceptable? Or: what are the grounds of scientistic rationalism? I will return to this question.

Let us now consider the moral argument against the doctrine of original sin. It points out that belief in a merciful and loving God is strikingly incongruous with His apparently bizarre, capricious and vengeful conduct as it is revealed in the myth of the fall of man, his exile, and redemption. If this argument has any foundations, then it should be asked – and inevitably this is the first question that the annals of Eden must provoke – how is it possible that millions of people have believed in a story which, on the rationalist account of it, glaringly defies all the principles of morality and of common sense handed down by the same teachers who have been responsible for perpetuating the history of Adam and Eve? The question whether or not it is just cruelly to punish mankind for a petty offence committed by an unknown couple in the remote past is not an intricate theological puzzle which can only be solved by highly trained logicians or lawyers; it is a problem easily accessible to illiterate peasants, and one wonders how people were induced to give credence to this kind of absurdity and why mankind had to wait for eye-openers Helvetius or Holbach before it would recognize its own amazing stupidity.

In fact, Christians have never been expected to believe in the story of the fall as retold and travestied by rationalists. It is not even material to genuine religious understanding whether or not they accepted in a literal sense the biblical account of what happened in the primeval garden. The history of Exile, one of the most powerful symbols through which people in various civilizations have tried to grasp, and to make sense of, their lot and their misery, is not a 'historical explanation' of the facts of life. It is the acknowledgement of our own guilt: in the myth of Exile we admit that evil is within us; it was not introduced by the first parents and then incomprehensibly imputed to us. If people had really been taught that Adam and Eve were responsible for all the horrors of human history, that unfortunate couple would surely have been cursed and hated throughout the history of Christianity; in fact their image in folklore has always been rather benign and sympathetic and their offence easily understandable: for who is permanently above temptation? Instead of devolving the responsibility for our misfortunes on a pair of ancestral figures we admit, through the symbol of our Exile, that we are cut out of warped wood (to use Kant's metaphor) and that we do not deserve to lead a carefree, happy and idle life; an admission that does not strike one as absurd.

The symbol of Exile includes, at the same time, a dim hope of Return to the lost home and a confidence that human suffering will not turn out to be in vain, after all, that something important has been gained on the human way of the Cross, which could not otherwise have been reached. The concept of *felix culpa* is the oblique anticipation of a Return which will bring something more than the restoration of pristine innocence; it implies that we do not simply revert to a previous state as if nothing had happened and that even the evil we have produced, or at least part of it, may have served as an instrument for our advancement.

This is the Christian narrative, of course, which includes, as well as the universal symbols of Exile and the Great Return, the story of Redemption. In the rationalist recasting, the latter is the preposterous tale of a God who delivered His innocent son to men so that they might torture him to death and as a result obtain forgiveness for their previous crimes. In reality the symbol of the Redeemer, though it implies the idea of justice, contains no suggestion of his punishment. It grew out of a metaphysics of evil, which, far from being a philosophical fabrication, was rooted, it seems, in the most ancient layers of mythology. This represents evil and suffering as being, so to speak, ontologically coupled, so that no evil fails to bring retribution. To take on suffering, of one's own free will and for the sake of others, is an act acceptable in all religions and in all moral codes which preserve the distinction between good and evil (although it is perhaps tautological to speak thus, since without this distinction it makes no sense to talk of morality any more).

The symbol of a suffering God who decides to share in full the fate of humans has at least two meanings. It affirms, firstly, the belief in a law of cosmic justice which operates figuratively speaking as a homeostatic mechanism: it requires suffering to restore the equilibrium undone by the destructive force of evil. Not only the actual debtor, but some other person may meet this demand on condition that he acts voluntarily; in other words, there may be shifts in the distribution of debits but only if these are freely accepted. The Sacrifice makes sense insofar as it fills the void an evil act has opened up in the mass of Being. The same symbol is, secondly, an avowal of our weakness; the human race needs a divine figure to repay the enormous debts it has incurred; lacking strength to acquit itself, it thereby confesses its moral infirmity. Yet in the same act of realizing its weakness mankind asserts its greatness and dignity: humanity is in God's eyes a treasure precious enough to deserve the descent of the divine Son into the world of flesh and pain, and the humiliating death he accepts for man's healing. Thus in the person of the Redeemer both the glorious and wretched sides of human existence are crystallized: a Pascalian theme *par excellence*. This ridiculous god, unable to save himself from ignominious death (so he was seen by the Jerusalem mob which derided his martyrdom and by pagan intellectuals like Celsus), this god was to become not only the most powerful symbol in religious history but a symbol whereby man gained a penetrating insight into his own destiny. Again, this is not merely philosophers' speculation: Jesus Christ who, in his person, in his life and suffering, in his *opprobrium* and in the ultimate triumph of his resurrection, testified both to the disgraceful misery and to the infinite dignity of man, is the real Jesus of simpletons' faith, the Jesus of carols and of popular paintings, an invincible heavenly protector and nevertheless a pauper like each of us.

Despair over the earthly or over something earthly is really despair about the eternal and over oneself, in so far as it is despair, for this is the formula for all despair. But the despairer . . . did not observe what was happening behind him, so to speak; he thinks he is in despair over something earthly and constantly talks about what he is in despair over, and yet he is in despair about the eternal.

Søren Kierkegaard, tr. W. Lowrie

To summarize this part of the discussion: an acceptance of the world as a divinely ordered cosmos wherein everything is given a meaning is neither self-contradictory nor inconsistent with empirical knowledge, and yet it can never be a consequence of such knowledge, however vastly expanded. Both moral evil and human suffering, including everybody's inevitable failure in life, can be accepted and mentally absorbed, but it would be preposterous to pretend that, starting with the terrifying chaos of life, we can, as a result of logically admissible procedures, end up with a cosmos full of sense and of purpose. The act of faith and trust in God has to precede the ability to see His hand in the course of events and in the sadness of human history. In brief: *credo ut intelligam.* Philosophical investigation is forever unable to produce, to replace, or even to encourage the act of faith, and probably nobody has ever been converted to faith by philosophical discussion except perhaps when the latter has served as an 'occasional', rather than an 'efficient' cause. At best, philosophical reflection might show that such acts of faith compel nobody to give credence, explicitly or otherwise, to beliefs which are incompatible with the known empirical facts or to belie moral notions accepted within the same creed – proviso being always made that 'faith' is not an act of intellectual assent to certain statements, but a moral commitment involving in one indivisible whole both intellectual assent and an infinite trust, immune to falsification by facts.

Oddly enough, the question which appears to be most embarrassing and most difficult to accommodate within a Christian theodicy arises from the fact of the suffering of animals. If human pain may be given a meaning in terms of sin, punishment, warning, trial, redemption, reward, the same cannot apply to animals; they are not morally guilty, they are not redeemed, they have no prospect of eternal life, yet they suffer. Why?

The question got a convenient, yet, alas, quite incredible solution from the orthodox Cartesians. Descartes' metaphysics did, indeed, entail that all kinds of acts involving sentience and perception take place in the immaterial soul, which has no mutual causal connection with the machine-body, and that to possess (or rather to be) a soul was the privilege of humans; animals, being non-sentient automata, simply do not suffer, no matter how much we are prompted by daily experience to fancy the opposite on the basis of misleading analogies. Animals cannot have been very happy about this philosophy, as the Cartesian physiologists, consistently enough, had no scruples about vivisection.

This doctrine does not seem to have been devised for the sake of coping with the theological riddle of animal pain; it was good for this purpose, but only contingently, and it was unacceptable, though for different reasons, both to Thomists and to Christian empiricists, like Gassendi.

Thus the unpleasant problem has remained without a credible solution and in fact failed to attract much attention from theologians, and not surprisingly: considering the amount of energy the problem of human suffering must have absorbed, not much was left over for rats, trout and shrimps. Still, at least two British Christian thinkers took up the issue. C. S. Lewis (in *The Problem of Pain*) devised a half-Cartesian solution. He states that one may attribute to animals sentience, but not consciousness, and this apparently means that although they suffer, they do not perceive the succession of particular moments of suffering, which therefore does not increase through the sheer continuity. How he got this insight into the animal psyche Lewis does not reveal. He seems to admit that animals do suffer but, lacking the continuing memory of pain, differently and less than people. Why they suffer at all has to be explained, though, and the most plausible hypothesis in Lewis's view is that the Devil corrupted the animal kingdom and incited the creatures to devour each other; this happened before man was created, and it was probably his task to restore good order, yet, having fallen himself, he failed to perform this duty. Since the animals do not have the kind of memory which can sustain a psychological identity, it is unlikely, according to Lewis, that God gave them the privilege of immortality: there is no way of resurrecting the same cat, simply because there is no feline 'sameness' in a psychological sense. Lewis does not, however, exclude the possibility that some pets might be eternalized, not for their own sake, but as components of resurrected human familial cells.

Peter Geach is strongly dissatisfied with this explanation. He thinks (in *Providence and Evil*) not only that Lewis's animal psychology has no foundation whatever but that it would not offer any solution even if it were true: provided, hypothetically, that animals have no perception of succession in their pain, they suffer all the same. And to devolve the responsibility for their pain on the Great Foe does not take it away from the Creator who must have given the proper permission, and thus is responsible as well; therefore Lewis's story, if true, would be an argument against God's goodness. Geach himself offers another view. There is simply no proof, he argues, that God, in His strategy for evolution, was interested at all in minimizing suffering; He appears rather not to be worried about animal or human pain. This does not contradict His perfection though, since most qualities which pass for virtues in humans (such as chastity, courage, even justice) make no sense when one is talking of God and He cannot be thought to share human compassion for others' physical discomfort.

If Lewis's image of a God who does not hinder Satan from tormenting animals denies the Creator's goodness, then how does Geach's own concept of a God who simply does not care about human and animal suffering leave His benevolence intact? This is a puzzle Geach does not try to explain. It seems that when we want to describe goodness, nothing is so essential as the will to save people (or animals) from suffering. A god who is simply indifferent cannot be the loving God of Christians. Perhaps Lewis's semi-Cartesianism which reduces animal pain to a barely perceptible level and traces its origin back to the wickedness of demons is not a bad suggestion, after all; and we might be happy with his solution if only he could give us a reason why it is true.

The question is probably much less urgent in Hindu wisdom where the borderline between men and other creatures has never been drawn so sharply, and the doctrine of metempsychosis implies that the same soul might in succession inhabit both animal and human bodies. And in Buddhist terms the question of suffering and of deliverance from it is the same, no matter who is the sufferer. Yet within Christian anthropology any suffering which can neither be redeemed nor explained in terms of punishment poses a distressing problem.

The Judaic and Christian world view, in contrast to the Eastern tradition, has never bothered much about lower creatures except in terms of human needs. Biblical man was given the right to master and to exploit the animals, and the Oriental idea of the unity and sanctity of all life (emphatically expressed in Jainism, yet present, it seems, in all the ramifications of Hinduism and Buddhism) has never been adopted in the mainstream of Christianity; by abrogating the Old Testament's alimentary taboos Christianity definitively removed the sacral qualities attached to the animal kingdom. St Francis conversing with brother wolf and St Antony of Padua preaching to sea fish in Rimini hardly embody the typical Christian attitude. Jesus himself did not seem to be much interested in non-human life except as a source of food and occasionally of material for a parable; he cast the devils out from an energumen and drove them into swine, he drove fish into the nets of fishermen and he cursed a sterile fig tree. It is arguable that by appointing man the lord of the earth and by subordinating Nature to his needs the Judaeo-Christian tradition encouraged the great thrust of technological and scientific progress on which Western civilization was to be built. Religions which preached the unity of life and an undifferentiated respect for it were not suited for prompting the technological conquest of matter.

CHAPTER 2

God of Reasoners

Religious ways of perceiving the world, institutions of worship, beliefs, are never born of analytical reasoning and need no 'proofs' of their veracity unless they are attacked on rational grounds. Logos in religion is a defensive weapon. The certainty of a believer is not that of a mathematician. The idea of proof worked out in such marvels of the human spirit as Plato's dialogues and Euclid's *Elements* was, of course, one of conditions for Western civilization, for both its scientific and legal achievements, yet it has played only a marginal role in its religious vicissitudes, all the monuments of Christian theology notwithstanding. Christianity was born as an apocalyptic awareness, as an appeal to all people to face the imminent *parousia* and to await the Kingdom in repentance, love and humility. Defiantly and proudly it opposed, in St Paul's messages, the unshakeable certainty of simpletons, their *stultitiam praedicationis*, to the mundane self-confidence of Alexandrian and Roman wiseacres. Soon, however, it had to take up the intellectual challenge; to conquer the urban educated elite it had to assimilate the weapon of natural Reason; and Christianity, as it has been developing since the end of the second century and as we now know it, is the result of encounter between two civilizations, a painful compromise between Athens and Jerusalem. The compromise has never been entirely happy and the intellectual

history of the Church has been plagued by incessant attempts
to challenge it from one side or another. Yet the Church has
displayed an admirable skill in preventing too wide a gap
between its intellectual effort and its foundation in faith. It
has kept philosophy in a subordinate position, stressing that
its great doctors were above all men of prayer and piety and
men of learning only secondarily; as the patron saints of
philosophers it appointed anti-philosophers: St Justin the
Martyr, who joined Christianity after a series of disappoint-
ments with all the Greek schools, and St Catherine of
Alexandria who, according to the legend, confuted fifty pagan
philosophers, aided by supernatural wisdom.

By not letting its intellectual elite be carried away by the
winds of autonomous Reason the Church, from the twelfth
century onwards, was bound to be accused of obscurantism.
However, in spite of a number of drastic mistakes, it showed
on the whole a sound intuition in strongly opposing all those
who tried to make the symbols of faith dependent on rational
arguments. Obviously, the *religio rationalis* of deists is
simply no religion at all. It is true that Christianity sustained
heavy losses from the Galileo affair, from the attack on the
theory of evolution, from its handling of the modernist crisis
and, in general, from all its conflicts with the Enlightenment
and modernity; yet one may safely say that it would simply
have disintegrated and disappeared had it made too many
concessions to the opposite side, had it not clearly and
obstinately refused to blur the borderline between the act of
faith and the act of intellectual assent; *had it not defined
itself by criteria which allowed of no distinction whatsoever between the culture of elites and that of paupers in
spirit.* No learning and no sophistication make anybody's
Christian faith better. The hubris of the highly educated has
always been severely castigated in all Christian churches.
Pascal perfectly summed up the issue by saying that the
Christian religion, being wise in that it has plenty of miracles
and prophecies to demonstrate its vigour, is foolish at the

same time, since it is not such things which make believers believe; only the Cross does.

Still, philosophical arguments, though reduced to a subsidiary role and never considered a foundation of faith, had an indispensable function in the self-defence of Christianity: the Catholic Church was eventually to condemn the doctrine that says God cannot be known with certainty by natural light (The First Vatican Council, *Canones de Revelatione*, 1).

What are we to make of the contention that natural light provides sufficient certainty of God's existence, i.e., a certainty that our reason is supposed to attain by starting from premises presumed to be empirical? Many traditional handbooks of Christian metaphysics list, next to the 'five ways' of St Thomas, a large number of other arguments all of which, in the opinion of the authors, either establish God's existence as an indisputable certainty or make it a highly plausible empirical hypothesis. All these arguments have been repeatedly attacked, either because they were logically unsound or because they implied false empirical presuppositions. However, some respectable Thomist authors (especially Manser) peremptorily state that no 'sixth way' is possible or desirable and that Aquinas' proofs are all we need to found a perfectly stable structure of natural theology.

Whether a thing is a blunder or not – it is a blunder in a particular system. Just as something is a blunder in a particular game and not in another.

Ludwig Wittgenstein

Let us try to sum up the crucial points of these arguments and refutations: a painful task if we bear in mind the countless number of theological and anti-theological works written on the subject.

St Thomas' arguments 'from the movement' and 'from

the efficient cause' have a similar logical structure. The former states that whatever moves is moved by something else and that the chain of movers has to have a first (and thus unmoving) link, since without it no second and therefore no subsequent movements would be possible. The argument from the efficient cause proceeds likewise: an infinite regression in the concatenation of causes is inconceivable since no second cause and thus no cause at all, could have operated if the first un-caused cause had not started the succession.

Apart from the fact that the Aristotelian premise implying that whatever moves is moved is untenable in terms of physics, the logical construction of both these cosmological arguments has always revealed, in critics' eyes, an incurable flaw. It seems to imply that if any link in a chain (of movements or of causes) has to be preceded by an earlier one, then there has to be the link preceding all of them. Clearly this is logically inadmissible, since from a statement having the form $\Pi x \Sigma y (y \rightarrow x)$, a statement with the reversed order of quantifiers (i.e., a statement of the form $\Sigma y \Pi x$ $(y \rightarrow x)$ may never be inferred (using the $\rightarrow$ sign to denote any kind of precedence, logical or physical). This is a mistake Kant pointed out when he opposed the rational postulate which demands that we look for the premise of any premise and for the condition of any condition to the false principle which states that the chain of syllogisms has an absolutely first premise or that the succession of conditions has an initial unconditioned term. In short, there is nothing logically wrong with the concept of an infinitive succession in the chain of events; no logical rules compel us to admit a first cause, whatever this cause might be.

A somewhat similar though not identical flaw appears in the argument 'from the degrees of perfection'. Here again, an impermissible leap from the succession of finite beings to actual infinity seems to be involved. The argument goes: since finite things differ from each other in their degree of perfection, we must conclude that there is a being which both embodies the maximum perfection conceivable and to which other beings owe their finite goodness. The argument seems, at first glance, particularly unconvincing; even if we knew how to measure and to compare the relative perfection of things, no conclusions could be drawn as to the necessary existence of something absolutely perfect, and still less as to this infinite perfection being the source of the relative one through an act of grace or of participation.

The teleological argument does not seem to be in a better position, even though the error lies in its quasi-empirical premise, rather than in faulty reasoning. It starts with the order of Nature which is so obviously dominated by a purposeful harmony that we cannot fail to perceive behind it the powerful mind of a wise organizer. This, at one time perhaps the most frequently employed of all arguments for the existence of God in popular Christian teaching, appears to be based on a fallacy which critics have repeatedly noticed, and which they did not need to wait for Darwin or Monod to unravel. It is arguable, indeed, that purposefulness is imposed on, rather than perceived in, organic nature. If we state that we perceive a purpose in an object we presuppose already conscious authorship and to reason *ex gubernatione rerum* to the existence of a Governor is, strictly speaking, to beg the question: to find a purpose is to find an author, prior to any reasoning. And the point is that within empirical investigation purposefulness, except for works of which the human authorship is previously known, may always be denied. The analogies used in popular Christian teaching – 'when we see a map we know that it took a mind to make it, thus it is absurd to deny the same about the earth itself which is depicted on the map!' – are utterly unconvincing. When we see a map, we know that a mind was at work to produce it precisely because there are no maps in nature and the actual physical topography of our globe offers no support whatsoever to this kind of reasoning.

The Darwinist explanatory framework interpreting organic phenomena might appear unsatisfactory to many scientists. Indeed, once it has been led to its ultimate consequences by Jacques Monod, it often strikes us as paradoxical: we naturally resist the idea that the entire evolution of living creatures, including our own species, is to be explained by an incredibly long series of random mechanical errors in copying the genetic code; within this scheme the existence of the human race, even given the initial conditions of life on earth, seems so fantastically improbable that for all practical and theoretical purposes we may safely dismiss it as an impossibility. And yet our reluctance might result from our inability to assimilate properly the rules of probabilistic thinking: we know, after all, that a mechanical shuffling of a pack of cards will always yield an arrangement of extremely small probability and nobody would risk a penny to bet on a particular order of fifty-two cards mixed by chance, i.e., on an event having the probability of $1 \div 1 \times 2 \times 3 \ldots 52$ (unless he cheats, that is). And so, a hypothetical mind living in another world might quite reasonably refuse to stake a penny on the chance of the existence of the human species in the solar system. He would lose after all, to be sure, because we happen to exist; yet his refusal would be perfectly rational. Extremely unlikely events occur every moment and it is not *a priori* more unthinkable that the evolution of life should be due to mere chance than that a particular order in a pack of cards should result from mechanical shuffling. If it turns out that rational creatures more or less similar to ourselves live somewhere in the universe, perhaps the entire body of neo-Darwinist thought will require a thorough revision, but even so one hardly sees how such a revision might conclusively establish the necessity of a divine watchmaker.

Surely many great physicists, when contemplating the incredibly complex order of matter, have felt that they could

Why does God not show Himself? – Are you worthy of it? – Yes. – You are presumptuous and thereby unworthy. – No. – And so, you are unworthy.

Blaise Pascal

not resist the idea of a Great Mathematician; that the structure of the universe must have originated in a mind and that we could not dispense with the idea of a constructor. But a consistent devil's advocate is hardly compelled to give in to such speculations. 'Physics is no doubt a work of mind,' – he would argue – 'but it is your mind, not God's. We, the human race, produced not only the instruments of measurement but the numbers as well, and we produced them in conformity with our biological structure and our specific organs of perception. We have no reliable evidence that the universe as it is, irrespective of our perceptions, contains any numerical relationships; we can never know – as a matter of principle, not of temporary deficiencies in our knowledge – how our contingent apparatus of seeing, touching, reacting to, and handling things contributes to the world picture which eventually emerges from the operation of our bodies and minds. Indeed to assess properly this contribution would amount to jumping out of our human skin, to getting rid of this contribution in the first place. It is not inconceivable that the universe is similar to our image of it, nor that God's spirit indeed hovers over the waters. Yet if this is the case, we cannot know it with any certainty, since our knowledge inevitably starts with and goes back to sense perception. Therefore our knowledge, vast as it may become, remains for ever within the brackets of our contingent position in the world, of our fundamental inability to acquire a non-relative vantage point (in the physical, biological, historical sense) for observing the World. The universe as we know it is the way we react to our environment, and our reactions are determined both biologically and culturally. We are understandably liable to see certain characteristics in the objects we perceive because these objects have indeed been shaped by our minds; hence we imagine that the world in and of itself operates according to certain differential equations, that it is built on well-defined quantitative relationships and is governed by purpose. A natural illusion, but an illusion all the same.'

Criticism of the kind illustrated by this hypothetical example does not necessarily imply a pragmatic idealism; it points out however that this sort of idealism cannot be refuted on the basis of experience or that attempts to disprove it along such lines involve a vicious circle; Kant and Husserl are in agreement up to this point.

Certainly, nothing in science prevents a physicist from believing in God, and his belief may find a psychological encouragement in his reflections upon the intricate machinery of Nature; yet he is not entitled to see this belief as an explanatory hypothesis in the scientific sense, let alone as a logical conclusion from a physical theory. Neither is he, by being a physicist, necessarily better equipped to tackle the question of God. Ultimately it is a matter of *Weltanschauung*, of philosophical or religious preference, no less in his than in anybody else's case. No one has ever heard of papers of God's existence being discussed at conferences of physicists; rightly so, as science offers no conceptual tools with which to tackle the problem.

And even if there were an intellectually legitimate path from the scientific world picture to a Great Calculator, the latter would be by no means the God of Christian faith (or of any religious faith), a benevolent protector who cares for all of us and for each of us separately. He would resemble rather some gigantic computer working perhaps with the utmost precision, yet remaining utterly indifferent to human destiny.

The same may be said, for that matter, of all the five ways

of St Thomas. Even if we assumed, wrongly, their logical validity, they would offer us the philosophers' God, not 'the God of Abraham and Isaac'. In the concept of the prime mover, of the first cause, of the *maxime ens*, of an absolute perfection and of the superior manager of the universe there is nothing necessarily entailing the quality of a fatherly curator who wants to save us, to protect us and eventually to give us the everlasting hospitality of His kingdom. This is not to say that the questions surrounding the philosophers' God are uninteresting or flimsy; they are simply irrelevant to what Christianity or any religion is about. Whether this God exists or not is hardly a religious issue, and is not a real worry to people to whom such issues matter. The God of philosophers is logically compatible both with the notion of an infinite computer and with the picture of a father who worries about His progeny and shares their suffering, but obviously only the latter is a person whom believers can worship, pray to, or even revolt against and revile. It is fair to add that St Thomas was well aware of this distinction and did not pretend that his arguments led us to the great Judge who had spoken to Moses from the burning bush. He realized that the core of Christianity was in revelation and he would never have uttered the delightful nonsense we owe to Father Garasse, the famous Jesuit polemicist and St Cyran's adversary, who averred that the proofs of God's existence were so cogent that it was as if we saw Him face to face. I would even venture to guess that St Thomas would not be happy with the equally nonsensical, though less delightful, expression 'scientific theology' (or rather *'wissenschaftliche Theologie'*) used sometimes by contemporary professors.

Still, since we keep trying to understand the philosophers' God, we have to mention two other proofs which, different though they might be from each other in their logical construction, both appeal to the fundamental distinction between 'the contingent' and 'the necessary': St Thomas' final demonstration and St Anselm's ontological argument.

The former boils down to this: all finite things, that is all things we can perceive, are contingent; this means they might exist or not; to put it in another way, there is nothing in their essence which necessarily entails their existence. If so, they cannot be everlasting and there must be a period of time when they do not exist. Therefore the entire collection of contingent things, and this means the world of matter and of spirits as a whole, could not conceivably exist had it not been created by a non-contingent, necessarily existing cause.

This argument is of particular importance because it involves a distinction the validity of which is arguably crucial for the 'to be or not to be' of metaphysics; this is not the case with concepts employed in the four Thomist arguments previously mentioned.

The distinction clearly cannot be established empirically and ever since Hume empiricists have, consistently enough, tended to reject it altogether (unless 'necessity' is conceived of as a property of analytical propositions). There is no

---

We want us to be necessary, inevitable, preordained since eternity. All the religions, almost all the philosophies, even a part of science, bear witness to the heroic, indefatigable effort of mankind to deny in despair its own contingency.

Jacques Monod

---

doubt that all empirical objects are corruptible, and we may even say that not many common-sense generalizations are more powerfully persuasive than this one. Yet the metaphysical concept of contingency implies not the physical corruptibility of particular agglomerations of matter but the corruptibility of the world as a whole. A necessary, ontologically self-supporting absolute is supposed to be compellingly postulated by the non-necessary, non-self-sufficient nature of the material Whole. Yet neither the Whole, nor its self-sufficiency or contingency are empirically founded ideas. St Thomas had in mind the image of a physical universe which was finite in space; and it has passed for certain since antiquity (both Democritus and Aristotle made the point) that spatial and temporal finitude were necessarily coupled and thus that a finite world could not enjoy everlastingness. However, the quality of contingency does not signify merely or mainly physical limitations and corruptibility; it refers to the very fact that the essence and the existence of a thing do not coincide, in other words that its essence does not involve its actual existence. The concept would still be valid in the hypothetical case of an immutable and eternal finite thing. And in saying that God's essence involves His existence the theologians usually do not mean a logical, but rather an ontic relationship; what they seek to say is not that once we know what God is we know that He cannot not exist, but rather that in reality He cannot not exist; or that God, and He alone, may be properly called the Being without qualifications.

To know properly what it is to be contingent in a metaphysical sense we have to know what it is to be non-contingent, thus to know what God is. The concept of contingency logically depends on its opposite and we may say that the argument *ex contingente et necessario* – not unlike the remaining four ways of St Thomas – only apparently proceeds from creatures to God. In fact it goes the other way round: we perceive the contingency of things once God's existence is known to us and not before. Therefore the Humean tradition refuses to legitimize the notion of contingency on the ground of its non-empirical character: we have no right to say that the world is contingent or that it is necessary in a theological sense.

It is fair to add that Thomists, when confronted with the logical objections to their arguments, occasionally concede that these might not meet the requirements of empirical

... All creatures are pure nothing. I do not say that they
are at least a little something but that they are pure
nothing, because no creature has being.
                                        Meister Eckhard, tr. R. B. Blakney

science but claim that they are valid nonetheless because
they employ metaphysical rules of reasoning. However,
there is little in this reply to convert an empiricist. 'There is
but one logic,' he would say, 'and its rules are universally
admitted in scientific inquiry. Within these rules the validity
of theological arguments is not granted and that is that.'

Nor will an empiricist be impressed by the famous
Cartesian reasoning. Descartes' claim is that he finds in his
own mind the concept of infinity and perfection and since his
mind is clearly imperfect and limited (the very act of
doubting reveals it, if indeed evidence is needed), it could
not possibly have fabricated this concept from its own
resources. Consequently the idea of the infinite being had to
be implanted in the human mind by another and more
powerful mind; considering that the effect has to be
commensurate to the cause, such a concept could not have
been formed if an infinite mind actually existing had not put
it there.

Empiricists find fault with this argument at two points.
The very concept of infinity, as Hobbes pointed out, is a
sheer negativity, an act of adding a particle of negation to
finite ideas; nothing corresponds to it in our experience and
nothing whatever suggests that we have an inborn idea of
infinity. Secondly, the principle demanding that the cause
be commensurate to the effect has no transparent meaning;
even less can it afford us any assurance that the idea of
infinity in our minds must have been causally produced by a
real infinite author.

There is, to be sure, something awkward in Descartes'

argument and within the rigours of empiricism it is bound to appear no more convincing than the Thomistic demonstrations. Descartes' reasoning differs from the Thomistic one in that it does not proceed from Nature to God; indeed, no such process is allowed for in his philosophy. Still, not unlike the scholastics he despised, he tried to discover within the finite world (that of a finite mind, though, not of finite physical things) a clue strongly, or even irresistibly, leading to infinity.

It appears then that both traditional Thomist proofs and Cartesian 'psychological' reasoning inevitably fall prey to Hume's critique: there is no logically sound path from the finite world to infinity.

Let us reflect for a moment upon the validity of this objection wherein all rationalist attacks on 'natural theology' are concentrated.

In daily life, in the practical manipulation of things, in scientific activity, we all think according to the same deductive and probabilistic logical rules, whether or not we are capable of articulating and codifying them, and apparently we have always done so. These rules in fact provide no tools which enable us to perform a miraculous leap from empirical data, however numerous, to infinity. Infinity, the empiricist tradition says, has no equivalent in experience. Indeed it has not. Yet neither has the idea of finitude. We do not perceive things as finite, unless we have in mind the idea of the opposite attribute, viz., of infinity. The two notions are mutually dependent in that neither is intelligible without a reference to the other; one does not need to be a structuralist to admit that. Even assuming that there is such a thing as a preconceptual perception, i.e., a perception in which abstract notions play no part (if it occurs, we have by definition no access to it), it cannot contain the quality of 'being finite'; and historically we know of no concept of finitude preceding that of infinity. Descartes, Spinoza, occasionally Hegel and often the pantheist writers, argued, against empiricists, that infinity is logically prior in the sense that we conceive of finite things as limitations or 'negations' of infinity (*omnis determinatio est negatio*) rather than of infinity as the mental extension or the denial of the finite. This is no doubt a metaphysical, and not a logical, issue; logically each term of the pair hinges on the other and so does the intelligibility of either. To assert the priority of infinitude is the same as to assert the contingency or non-self-sufficiency of the finite world, and the real question is: where does this idea come from? Neither Descartes nor Spinoza could, within the conceptual framework of their thinking, accept any cosmological arguments, any logical ladder starting with the objects of daily life, with their causal connections, their variety, their purposeful order, etc., and leading to the perfect world-manufacturer. However, their thought was clearly stimulated by the shared feeling that the world we know within the limited horizon of our experience is not self-explanatory or even (in a sense to be discussed presently) that it is irreal, that its very presence begets the questions 'what is it?' and 'why is it?'.

These are not scientific questions in the sense in which the word 'science' has been used during the last two centuries. Yet it by no means follows from this admission that they are meaningless, empty, absurd, pre-logical, and so on: epitaphs under which the advocates of scientistic ideology have endeavoured to bury them. Such questions, and in particular the most fundamental among them, the one crucial both to Leibniz and to Heidegger – 'why is there something rather than nothing?' – are expressions of what is misleadingly labelled metaphysical experience. The label is misleading insofar as the word 'metaphysical' strongly suggests a reference to ready-made philosophical doctrine, whereas in fact such doctrines are generated by, rather than preceding, this kind of experience. People – and by no means professional philosophers only – often have experiences which they describe as astonishment at the fact of existence,

> Our life is nothing but impossibility, absurdity. Every
> thing we desire is contradictory to the conditions or
> consequences attached to it; every statement we make
> implies its contradiction; all of our feelings are mixed up
> with their opposites, because we are made of contradic-
> tion, being creatures and at the same time God, and at the
> same time infinitely other than God.
>
> *Simone Weil, tr. T. R. Nevin*

awe in face of 'Nothingness', apprehension of the unreality
of the world or the feeling that whatever is impermanent
must be accounted for by what is indestructible. Experiences of this kind are not mystical in the strict sense, i.e.,
not events people interpret as direct encounters with God.
They might rather be described as a strong feeling that in the
fact of being and of not being – in this very fact and not only
in the experiencing person's existence – there is something
unobvious, alarming, puzzling, queer, astounding, something which defies all the ordinary, daily norms of understanding. Such feelings cannot be and need not be converted
into scientific 'problems'; they are expressed, more or less
clumsily, as metaphysical riddles. There is in them no stuff
for 'proving' anything if 'to prove' retains the sense it usually
has in scientific procedures. Indeed, inserted as links into a
chain of reasoning they usually look poor and unconvincing.
Yet it is astonishingly foolish to dismiss them, as empiricists
often do, as errors generated by the wrong usage of words or
subject to explanation as an abuse of semantic standards.

Both metaphysical experience (if we stick to this ill-
devised term) and faith based on revelation suffer a deep
corruption when they are articulated in the idioms of
philosophical and theological speculation and when philosophers try to cram them into forms simulating those of
natural science. The labour of the human spirit as it wrestles

> . . . A part of metaphysics gravitates, consciously or
> otherwise, around the question why something exists: why
> matter or why spirits or why God, rather than nothing?
> However, this question implies that reality fills a void, that
> there is nothingness underneath being, that in principle
> nothing should exist and that therefore one has to explain
> why in fact there is something. Such a preoccupation is a
> pure illusion, for the idea of an absolute nothingness has
> as much meaning as the idea of a square circle.
>
> *Henri Bergson*

with this peculiar kind of experience does not need to be included in, or confused with, the human effort to predict, to explain and to manipulate physical events. Still, these two inevitably have something in common: their claims to truth. We shall soon discuss this common ground.

Metaphysical speculations arising from astonishment at being and not-being, not unlike theological assertions expressing faith built on revelation, are bound to be unconvincing to those who do not share in this kind of experience nor participate in this mythological tradition. But to convince is really not the point. Did St Thomas in fact try to convince the atheists (few and far between in those days) that God existed? Did Descartes, even though an atheist was less of a rarity in the seventeenth than in the thirteenth century? One may doubt it. The former tried to polish up the available conceptual apparatus in order to translate his faith into Aristotelian parlance; the latter worked out his experience of the unreality of the world, whose reality he wanted to restore by the only possible, although roundabout, route which led from his own self-awareness to God, and from thence to Nature. Descartes found no traces of God in the physical machinery of the universe, let alone in the wealth of its life-forms (and life was to him nothing but a particular case of the operation of mechanical laws); he underwent an experience in which the non-existence of the world appeared to him a distinct possibility. St Thomas looked at a world which teemed with God's signs: he saw them in the light of his spiritual heritage. In spite of the utterly dissimilar logical structure of their respective arguments, both perceived the impossibility of a world thrown back upon itself (never mind that, historically, Cartesianism was one of the major sources of modern atheism).

They produced no 'proofs' in the modern sense. There is no proof starting with 'everything' or 'nothing' and showing that 'everything' we know from experience is in fact nothing if we suppose it is everything.

In other words, as long as we comply with the logical rigour acceptable in scientific inquiry, there are no traces of God unmistakably detectable in the world, nothing we could identify with certainty as His signs. This might emerge more clearly if we ask the following question: let us suppose that God, exasperated by our mushrooming incredulity, decides

---

God made also man after his own image and likeness, in the mind: for in that is the image of God. This is the reason why the mind cannot be comprehended even by itself, because in it is the image of God.

St Augustine, tr. H. Browne

---

to supply the human race with irrefutable proofs of His existence, without however applying any mental compulsion, i.e., without infusing into our minds the irresistible grace of faith (which He can and does do according to Calvinist, although not to Catholic, theology). He will only perform an act which any rational and scientifically disposed mind must unambiguously interpret as His sign. What could He do? What sort of extraordinary miracles might He perform in which nobody of sane mind could fail to perceive His hand? It is easy to realize that He could do nothing of this kind. A well-trained sceptic may see with his own eyes all the miracles reported in Jacques de Voragine's *Golden Legend* and remain as untouched as a stone in his incredulity. He may always plausibly state that any natural explanation, however unlikely, of the supposed miracles is more likely, after all, than an explanation in terms of God's interventions. This is a *quaestio iuris*, not *facti*: the point is not that some inveterate sceptics might, in fact, foolishly turn their eyes away from the irresistible evidence, but that they would have a perfect right to do so in terms of the intellectual patterns of modern knowledge which simply cannot assimilate such an event as a 'miracle'. Consequently one is bound, in terms of this way of thinking, to assume that any explanation from 'natural' causes, no matter how implausible, is better than a supernatural one. (Spinoza did not deny the factual truth of the story of how the Jews crossed the Red Sea; he just believed, or pretended to believe, that an extremely strong wind caused by a natural chain of events might have parted the waters and opened the passage to the refugees.)

Thus the deity is without form and nameless. Though we ascribe names, they are not to be taken in their strict meaning; when we call him One, Good, Mind, Existence, Father, God, Creator, Lord, we are not conferring a name on him . . . He cannot be comprehended by knowledge, which is based on previously known truths, whereas nothing can precede what is self-existent. It remains that the Unknown be apprehended by divine grace and the Word proceeding from him.

> **St Clement of Alexandria, tr. H. Bettenson**

Thus God is helpless to produce any empirical evidence for His existence which would seem irrefutable, or even highly plausible, in scientific terms; to assert this by no means amounts to restricting His omnipotence because to overcome the difficulty He would have to perform a logical, rather than a physical, miracle, and His inability to do so is compatible with, or even included in, the very nature of omnipotence (I have discussed this question earlier on). He certainly could impose faith on people, acting directly on their souls, yet on the assumption that He follows a non-totalitarian line in matters of faith and forbears to use mental coercion directly, He is powerless to break the justified resistance of a consistent sceptic.

On the other hand a sceptic is himself powerless to crush the obstinacy of a consistent believer, and this again is a *quaestio iuris*, not *facti*. The believer has a perfect right to be incorrigible and insensitive to the sceptic's arguments. He sees the signs of God's presence in his and in other people's lives, in historical events, in the natural order, and he is ready to admit that his faith precedes his acts of reading these signs, not the other way round. In other words, he recognizes that his faith is faith, rather than a result of the scientific examination of evidence. He might refer to a special kind of experience or of enlightenment whose validity the sceptic refuses to acknowledge.

'My certainty,' he says, 'far from being a set of gratuitously accepted beliefs, is rooted in a perception which produces a coherent image of the world. All people who share a similar experience understand each other without difficulty and if you refuse to admit their testimony this is because you lack the corresponding faculty, or rather lack the will to acquire it. People with normal hearing can communicate in a perfectly intelligible language in matters concerning music, yet a person born deaf would find their words meaningless.'

'The analogy does not hold good', the sceptic replies. 'In your opinion faith is of utmost importance to the way in which God rules his human subjects. So why should He give this particular faculty to some people while refusing it to others? Why am I unable to see what you claim to see?'

'You can,' the believer replies, 'if you wish. There is no compulsory faith in God's dealings with people, just encouragement. This is ultimately a matter of will, rather than of cognitive effort.'

'Then you admit that you cannot convince me?'

'Quite so. I cannot.'

'But you claim your faith to have a cognitive value, you pretend to know a truth which is inaccessible to me. Consequently, your position is self-defeating if you have no means to convince me on cognitive grounds.'

'This depends on what is meant by cognitive grounds. How do you define mental acts leading to gains you accept as cognitively valid?'

'Those acts are defined in scientific procedures. To be sure, long discussions have been going on about how precisely to define what is or is not justified in empirical science, and many litigious points remain. And yet in most cases scientists are able to communicate and to assess the validity of their work and they normally agree that there is a vast area of speculation which does not deserve their attention because nothing said in this area can even remotely meet their standards, however imprecisely defined. Therefore they do not discuss the question of miracles, of angels, of God.'

'But what might convince me that the criteria applied in modern scientific investigation are at the same time criteria discriminating between what has or has not cognitive value, let alone between what is or is not meaningful?'

'That is easy to answer. Scientific method can predict what will happen. For instance, if I use a well-defined force to throw a well-defined body in well-defined gravitational conditions, I can calculate the relevant factors and demonstrate the correctness of the prediction. I can describe how a living cell is able to reproduce itself, I can foresee when a solar eclipse will occur and I can tell you what is the chance of your winning at a gambling table. The methods are more reliable in some fields and less so in others, of course, and we know why this is so; but the conditions of scientific achievement are clear enough, all philosophic quarrels about verifiability and falsifiability notwithstanding. You cannot use your skill in divinity in the same manner to predict, to make, to calculate, to explain. The most magnificent temples were built on the basis of engineers' calculations, not on their prayers; otherwise they would have never been constructed, or they would have fallen apart.'

'You miss the point completely' – is the believer's rejoinder. 'Nobody pretends that faith might replace scientific knowledge or that one may pray instead of working and get the same results; indeed, Christianity explicitly made illicit this kind of illusion. My question was on what grounds do you assert, as you clearly do, that what we know is restricted to what we can justify in terms of methods acceptable in modern science, however exactly or inexactly defined?'

'Precisely on the grounds that scientific methods prove to be reliable in predicting events and can be practically applied with considerable success, which religious beliefs may not claim to do.'

'We are going round in a circle. I am asking where this concept of knowledge or of cognitive value comes from. On what grounds is a knowledge which fails to meet these requirements excluded?'

'We may not have ultimate reasons but we see that everyone can ultimately be convinced about truth in science because a broad agreement has been reached as to the criteria of validity. This is not the case in religious matters. You cannot persuade me to accept your beliefs, but we can convince each other on questions which are amenable to solution by scientific methods.'

'Yes, but you cannot convince me as to your fundamental premise: the exclusive right your criteria possess to define what knowledge is.'

'Even if I cannot, these criteria are universally accepted, whereas in religious questions – which I maintain are no questions at all – there is no commonly accepted way of judging and solving the issues under discussion.'

'Then it all boils down to a matter of majority opinion or of *consensus omnium?*'

'So be it; that does not bother me at all!'

The result of the controversy is not totally empty. The believer and the sceptic have no way of convincing each other, and their incapacity and doggedness reveal that their respective epistemological decisions are irreducibly different with no supreme judge in sight. That no criteria of validity can be established without a vicious circle has been, of course, a banal philosophical topic since Sextus Empiricus; yet the antiquity of this topic has failed to enfeeble it. In fact the sceptic who appeared in the above dialogue is only a half-sceptic: he is rather an adherent of scientistic philosophy. He is not sceptical about the legitimacy of criteria employed in scientific investigations, he simply does not worry about their ultimate justification or a possible *petitio principii* so long as they prove successful, and this means, so long as the body of science keeps working for the purpose which it emerged in our civilization to work for. Whether there is only one purpose and, above all, whether this purpose has remained immutable throughout the history of science, is a highly debatable question which is beyond the scope of this discussion. Setting it aside, we may still ask: are we to believe that science is indeed fulfilling its task and that this is what constitutes the foundation of its cognitive validity? Is to be, to be valid? If we admit this (Hegelian, rather than scientistic, and somewhat desperate) principle, there is no reason why it should not apply to religious beliefs as well. Meanwhile this is what the half-sceptic in the dialogue above denies. He supports the claim to truth within science, yet not within beliefs based either on the peculiar experience of the Sacred or on the authority of a mythological tradition. Therefore to escape from this impasse we must confront the most basic and the oldest philosophic question: what possible foundation has any claim to truth?

I will try to argue for the following, quasi-Cartesian assertion: Dostoyevski's famous dictum, 'If there is no God, everything is permissible', is valid not only as a moral rule (I will discuss this point somewhat later) but also as an epistemological principle. This means that the legitimate use of the concept 'truth' or the belief that 'truth' may even be justifiably predicated on our knowledge is possible only on the assumption of an absolute Mind.

The claim is by no means new. It may be called quasi-Cartesian insofar as it takes up the core of Descartes' hypothesis of a devilish impostor and his contention that the perfection of an absolute being is a condition of truth. The argument is not Cartesian, though.

I shall stick to the semantic notion of 'true' without discussing Heidegger's tenet to the effect that a sentence is not necessarily or mainly 'the place' of truth (i.e., that there are no reasons to restrict the prediction of truth to sentences only). There is no 'genuine' sense of 'truth' which we can uncover in the etymology of the Greek word and confront with the allegedly distorted sense that the concept acquired in Latin and in other tongues. To be sure, nothing prevents us from employing the metaphysical (as opposed to the epistemological) concept of truth in conformity with the scholastic, Spinozist or Hegelian tradition, yet we may not assert that this is the only authentic or permissible concept, even if it in fact accords with a forgotten or half-forgotten linguistic usage.

The everyday semantic concept of truth is transcendental

in the early-Husserlian (not in the scholastic) sense; in other words, in attributing the property of truth to an utterance we presume that something is the case as stated in the utterance and that it is the case whether or not the utterance is ever or ever will be made, whether or not its

---

What we think and say is true or false according to what the thing is or is not. But when the intellect is the cause and rule of things, truth consists in the conformity of the thing to the intellect. The work of an artist, for example, is said to be true when it conforms to his art. Now just works bear the same relation to the law which they obey as do works of art to the art itself. God's justice is therefore rightly called truth, because it determines the order of things in conformity with his wisdom, which is its law. We ourselves speak of the truth of justice, in the same sense.
St Thomas Aquinas, tr. A. M. Fairweather

---

truth is ever or ever will be confirmed; what is true is so irrespective of whether we know or ever will know that it is true, whether or not we think of it, whether or not we exist, whether or not any cognitive acts occur now or ever.

Throughout the history of scepticism and of empiricism the legitimacy of this concept has been questioned. It has been repeatedly pointed out that the signs whereby we recognize truth and falsity are governed by normative rules which in their turn require justification; these rules cannot be inferred from the empirical material which, precisely, is subject to epistemological examination. Therefore, in defining an operative notion of truth we face an unpleasant choice: either an infinite regress or a discretionary decision, and in the latter case everything is indeed permissible. Consequently an empirical epistemology founded on psychological or physiological investigation is in principle, and not just contingently, 'inconceivable'; strictly speaking it is an absurdity.

The expression 'discretionary decision' refers to the logical, not the historical, situation. It is not impossible to explain in historical and causal terms the process by which the criteria of cognitive validity have been worked out and codified in the form of probabilistic logic. Still, such decisions are discretionary in the sense that none can be justified without a vicious circle.

And so, when we invoke the efficacy of science in order to legitimize its more or less codified criteria of validity, our appeal has no epistemological relevance and leaves intact all the sceptical arguments about the fundamental unreliability of all criteria of truth, even if we set aside the well-known difficulties of properly defining the principle of verifiability and are satisfied with the general guidelines of scientific empiricism. There are no transcendental or logically compelling grounds to take the efficacy of knowledge (its predictive power and practical applicability) as a mark of truth in the sense just mentioned. We may certainly define truth by reference to the criteria of efficacy; such a definition is not self-contradictory and does not lead into an infinite regress; nevertheless it is arbitrary; to accept it requires an act of faith and therefore the principle *credo ut intelligam* operates over the entire field of knowledge; this is hardly more than to say that we are incapable of producing an epistemological absolute or that our intelligence is finite: not exactly a world-shaking discovery.

This discovery has little to do with the needs and with the development of science, which requires norms of acceptability and not of truth in the transcendental sense. Occasionally, in moments of crisis, when its metaphysical or anti-metaphysical background is suddenly revealed, science looks for a philosophical self-justification, yet logically it does not need to presuppose that what is acceptable according to its criteria should also be true. Should this last predicate be dropped or forgotten, the efficacy of empirical knowledge is not thereby altered. And if anybody denies legitimacy to the generally admitted criteria of acceptability, he cannot be convinced that he is wrong by any logically cogent arguments. In short, an epistemological nihilism or an unrestricted licentiousness is empirically invincible.

Among the arguments which used to be advanced against this sceptical reasoning the most important is this: a sceptical standpoint cannot consistently be upheld; when a sceptic says 'nothing is true' he means 'it is true that nothing is true'; thus his position is self-defeating as the result of an inescapable contradiction. Thus the early Husserl.

This counter-argument is hardly convincing. A sceptic by no means feels compelled to say 'it is true that nothing is true'. He may well be satisfied with contending that the predicate 'true' is needless and its use unjustifiable. He simply rejects the equation stating that the sentence 'the sun shines' is equivalent to the sentence 'it is true that the sun shines'. If he is consistent, he has to get rid of the temptation to ascribe to his words any truth-value or cognitive meaning. His attitude is that no claims to truth are implied in speech acts. Speaking consists in practical actions whereby people try to gain or to avoid something. It has certainly been a long-standing habit to endow those actions with additional values of truth and falsity, yet the longevity of this habit does not make it any the more legitimate. And the question 'why do some of those acts turn out to be practically efficacious while others lead to defeat?' is unanswerable if it implies any metaphysical correspondence between the content of our speech acts and the world in itself.

Consequently, the sceptic's attitude is that we ought to stop worrying about how to justify the concept of truth and should instead abandon epistemological inquiry altogether, unless we can find access to an epistemological Absolute: this was clear both to Descartes and to Husserl. After Kant,

Husserl's was the boldest and the deepest-drilling philosophical machine to seek the well of ultimate certainty without
God; however far his bore might have progressed in
uncovering the hidden layers of consciousness, it could not
work endlessly and all the results were bound to be open to
doubt. There was no last and definitive ground of which one
did not need to ask 'what is *its* ground?', no proverbial
ultimate whale supporting the turtle which supported the
earth. No final answer could be found to the question 'how do
we know that the transcendental Ego is infallible?' The point
is not that it is more difficult to contrive a 'proof' of the
transcendental Ego's existence than of God's, but that the
former, having no ontological status of its own and thus no
divine self-grounding identity, cannot conceivably be freed
from the contingency and uncertainty of human empirical
consciousness. On the assumption that there is such a
perfect, original and primordial insight, unpolluted by the
psychological, biological and historical contingency of the
human mind, it may take one of three forms: a new
pseudonym for God (which Husserl clearly does not want it
to be), a pure absolute standpoint without a subject (which
means a kind of grinning without a cat) or else a discoverable
property of the psychological Ego, sharing the latter's
fallibility. Perhaps an unerring insight is conceivable in the
pure immanence of a self-regarding Ego, but in this context
even the expression 'self-regarding' seems improper considering that we cannot imagine a consciousness seeing itself
without the intermediary of a mirror; we should talk of self-
identity, rather than of self-regard, and if so, the cognitive
perfection of such a consciousness would be of no use to us
mortals, since whatever it tried to communicate to us would
inevitably pass through the polluting medium of our
'psychological Ego' and of our speech and thus be infected
with their contingency. And if there is something in us like
'the spark of God' – in Meister Eckhart's words – it cannot
be there without God who subsists irrespective of our

knowledge of Him. Husserl's attempt to uncover a path which leads to truth (i.e., infallibility) while by-passing God is therefore as unreliable as all other such philosophic endeavours; it is vain to hunt for a godless certainty and therefore vain to hunt for truth *tout court.*

As rivers flowing downwards find their home
In the ocean, leaving name and form behind,
So does the man who knows, from name and form
    released,
Draw near to the divine Person who is beyond the beyond.
Whoever really knows the all-highest Brahman, really
Becomes Brahman.
                    From: Mundaka Upanishad, *tr. R. C. Zaehner*

This is what Descartes, unlike Husserl, was aware of. And yet his reasoning to the effect that we may trust our cognitive powers by relying on God's veracity is far from convincing, not only because his arguments for God's existence are faulty but because he supposed the reliability of our perception and of our logical instruments to be based on God's *moral* perfection and on the resulting certainty that He cannot deceive us. But God's goodness and omniscience do not necessarily entail that He can never lead us into error. It may not *a priori* be excluded that truth, let alone the whole truth, is harmful to imperfect creatures and that in some cases it is good for us to be misinformed. In any case there is nothing obvious about the assumption that the truth cannot conflict with other goods; this ought to be proved separately. God's veracity, taken as a foundation of the reliability of knowledge, in fact piles up new difficulties: the very possibility of error becomes unintelligible and Descartes' proposal that we should devolve responsibility for error on the will (since error cannot be included in acts of cognition, only in acts of will affirming what reason does not authorize us to affirm) seems weak and artificial.

However, the Cartesian idea can be made to appear sound if we reduce it to a more general form which says: without the absolute subject the use of the predicate 'true' may not be validated.

This by no means implies that by assuming an absolute subject we can know where the truth lies and how to tell it from error. What we have in mind is a logically prior question; we do not ask about the criteria of truth, we want to know what the legitimate use of the concept necessarily implies. The mere knowledge of God's existence does not tell us what is true yet arguably it does tell us that something is.

If the sceptics' arguments are valid, the idea of truth is indefensible, indeed meaningless. In order that something be true, a subject that cannot err has to exist. This subject has to be omniscient; we cannot conceive a subject that would possess a fragmentary knowledge but enjoy within this a perfect certitude. No partial truth can carry an absolute certitude unless it is related to the whole truth; otherwise the meaning of the partial truth must always remain in doubt: the owner of a partial truth can neither know how the truth beyond his reach might alter the sense of the truth he has taken possession of nor what the latter's scope of validity is.

Thus, without the all-encompassing truth there is no fragmentary one; and the all-encompassing truth pre-supposes an infinite omniscient intelligence. It alone might fulfil what Husserl expected from a transcendental Ego.

However in the omniscient mind, by definition, the distinction between subject and object is abrogated, as absolute knowledge implies a perfect transparence; in other words, such a subject has to *be* all it knows. Consequently, to it (or to Him) there is no truth in the sense in which the word is applied to human knowledge, where the distinction between the perceiver and what is perceived must always remain in force. This is what Christian metaphysics asserts by saying that God, strictly speaking, does not know truth but *is* truth and that in him indeed *esse et verum convertuntur* (I leave aside the question of what the same assertion might mean when it is derivatively applied to the creatures). And the very definition of an omniscient mind implies its perfect actuality: the distinction is abolished both between what is and what could be, and between what was, what is and what will be; otherwise it would know itself and things by the intermediary of memory and of anticipation and therefore would no longer be the all-embracing truth.

... For in eternity there is no yesterday nor any tomorrow, but only Now.

Meister Eckhart, tr. R. B. Blakney

Thus I follow the Cartesian formula insofar as it asserts that human claims to truth are empty without reference to the divine being. No reference to God's veracity is thereby implied; but I admit that the predicate 'true' has no meaning unless referred to the all-encompassing truth, which is equivalent to an absolute mind. The transcendental approach is thus far vindicated.

The argument has nothing to do however with the proofs of God's reality: it can neither reinforce nor enfeeble any of the arguments in existence. Its aim is not to show that God does exist, but to expose the dilemma which we seem to face when we cope with the question of truth and of the very possibility of an epistemology: either God or a cognitive nihilism, there is nothing in between.

I have been trying to argue that God is not and cannot be an empirical hypothesis and that there are no identifiable signs of His presence if the word 'hypothesis' retains its usual sense. His presence cannot explain anything in particular – again in the usual sense of the word 'explain' – and the question 'how to explain everything?' may be

Nowhere in the world can God be found. He escapes embodied presence and perception. His reality is not in space and time. His existence cannot be demonstrated. His reality, if it is, has to be of a radically different character from the reality of the world. No science in the sense of a universally valid God-cognition develops from thinking of God, no cognition which might investigate the object 'God'. For there is no God to the knowledge.

Karl Jaspers

dismissed on the ground that 'everything' is not a concept that can be properly constructed. Whether or not it is so is a matter of philosophical preference: it is plausible to argue that once the 'explanation of everything' is recognized as a possible task, the quest for an absolute Being becomes intellectually inescapable. But not only are there no compelling reasons to recognize the possibility of such a task; there are strong motifs against recognizing it within the conceptual framework of modern science. This might not bother the believer at all; yet a believer should and may admit, firstly, that his interest goes beyond the boundaries of legitimacy as defined, however loosely, in science; secondly, that even assuming the explanatory power of an absolute Being we would be very far away (perhaps infinitely far away) from the God of believers, a friend and a father; thirdly, that any explanation would be in any case extremely doubtful given the insurmountable difficulties of making the idea of creation intelligible: the gap between the absolute Being and the collection of finite things would still not be bridged.

There is a way of attempting to find an intellectual path to God which would not imply any assumptions about the finite world; here the point is to show that we cannot consistently think of God while denying His existence. This attempt is known as the ontological argument. It seems to have provoked more controversies among philosophers throughout the centuries than any other component of natural theology. Perhaps the reason why it has been so hotly debated was that anybody getting acquainted with it for the first time was usually struck by the feeling both of an obvious fallacy and of an irritating difficulty in saying where exactly the fallacy lay.

. . . He who cannot be grasped or comprehended or seen makes himself seen, comprehended and grasped by those who believe, that he may give life to those who grasp and see him by faith . . . True life comes from partaking in God; and to partake in God is to know him and to enjoy his goodness.

St Irenaeus, tr. H. Bettenson

The core of St Anselm's ontological argument is that God is a being nothing greater than which can be conceived; to suppose that God exists merely in our mind, and not in reality, would amount to stating that He is not the greatest being conceivable because to exist really is greater than to exist in mind only. In other words, according to St Anselm, whoever accepts (as everyone does) this concept of God and denies His existence contradicts himself, since to deny God's real existence is to reject the definition of Him as the most perfect being conceivable, and thus as an existing being.

The critics' main counter-argument may be summed up by saying that St Anselm includes existence in the definition of God and then declares that it is self-contradictory to admit the definition while professing atheism: it is indeed self-contradictory but only because of the illicit definition; you might likewise fancy a definition of the kind 'Pegasus is an existing winged horse' and then argue on this basis that Pegasus is a real animal.

The matter is certainly less simple than this counter-argument suggests. St Anselm would not have applied his reasoning to Pegasus or to anything else save God precisely because there is conceivably only one being '*quo maius cogitari nequit*'. He does not say in this context that God's essence involves His existence, but this is what he must have in mind in stating the definition. The nerve of the argument lies in the idea that we cannot think of God as an imaginary entity once we know what it is to be God: viz. a being which cannot not exist. Thus the argument might be perhaps rephrased by saying that if God is conceivable at all, He cannot not exist. This is roughly how our contemporary defender of St Anselm, Charles Hartshorne, tackles the issue; in his view the ontological argument is perfectly reasonable if restated as a hypothetical judgement: 'if God is possible, God is necessary'.

But is God conceivable on the assumption that to conceive Him is to admit that His essence and existence converge and thus that He is a necessary being not only in the sense that He happens to exist, eternally and immutably, but in the sense that He is bound to exist, is *causa sui*, so that His non-existence would be, as it were, an ontic contradiction?

It is proper to add that one may consistently admit the concept of God's essence involving His existence and reject the ontological argument; this is what St Thomas and his followers, among others, did. The reason why the Thomists resisted the argument was that it seemed to endow our fallible intellect with too much power: we *can*, as a matter of fact, conceive God as non-existent, the Thomists say, not because His existence is not really included in His essence but because of the weakness of our reason; in short, we are so feeble-minded that we can be atheists. One may suspect, even though St Thomas does not say so in so many words, that St Anselm's reasoning displayed a kind of intellectual hubris, an impermissible confidence in the prowess of philosophy; in Thomistic terms the only way to God within the reach of natural light (i.e., apart from revelation and the rare gift of mystical union) starts with the imperfection and non-self-sufficiency of creatures, and not from our knowledge of God's nature. Perhaps it would even be proper to say that to the Thomists the ontological argument is true but that only God can understand its truth (which, however, seems to lead us into antinomy, as a statement of the form 'A is true but only God can know that' implies 'I know that A is true but I cannot know that it is'. Thus the content of the sentence would be negated by the act of uttering it not unlike what would happen if we were to say 'I am unable to speak a single word of English' or 'I am mute'.) Thomistic arguments show a world which requires God in order to be what it is; they do not reveal God's impenetrable and independent nature.

Kantian and positivistic criticism of the ontological argument is more radical. Kant's formula that 'existence is no real predicate' implies that there is no distinction between saying 'I am thinking of God' and 'I am thinking of the existing God' unless the latter combines the two logically independent statements, 'I am thinking of God' and 'God exists', in which case the last sentence needs a separate justification. Anselm's reasoning however is to show that in one and only one case saying 'I am thinking of A' equals 'I am thinking of the existing A', and that the latter does not equal 'I am thinking that A exists' but 'while I am thinking of A I cannot think it does not exist'.

According to Kantian and Humean tradition the fallacy of the ontological argument consists in its seeking to prove that the judgement 'God exists' is analytically true, whereas no judgement may be both analytically true and existential in content. Why not?

To discuss this question thoroughly I should have to venture into the large field of the long-standing controversy over the definition of analycity. I do not feel competent to take on the task, and I leave aside the arguments of various modern philosophers to the effect that no analytical judgement can be valid unless it implies an existential presupposition (Poincaré and Le Roy started this; Schlick and Ajdukiewicz followed); if these arguments are solid they should call for a modification of the principle just mentioned but they would not vindicate the legitimacy of the concept of 'necessary being' or confirm the soundness of St Anselm's proof.

Yet we may look for an *instantia crucis* and ask if there is another example of a judgement which would combine these two properties – incompatible in Kantian and Humean terms – i.e., which would be analytic and existential in content. A candidate for this impossible chimera is, I suspect, the judgement 'something exists'. The reason why this judgement might be said to be analytic and thus 'necessary' is that its negation 'nothing exists' is not just false but unintelligible and absurd: indeed, if anything is absurd, this is. On this assumption one may argue that 'something exists' is equal to 'necessarily something exists'. One is tempted to equate this last statement with 'something exists necessarily', which would amount to the Anselmian claim: the very idea of existence leads to the conclusion that there is a necessary being. It is true, though, that it is illicit, in terms of modal logic, to infer 'something exists necessarily' from 'necessarily something exists'. If such an inference is impermissible, it follows that we may consistently uphold the latter and deny the former, i.e., that it is consistent to say 'necessarily something exists but nothing exists necessarily'.

It seems that we are now thrown back on the problem of the contingency of the world; we might be incapable of conceiving 'the non-existence of the world', i.e., total 'nothingness', and thus be entitled to believe that 'necessarily something exists' and still maintain that whatever exists, whether taken separately or as a whole, is contingent. No logical rules can settle this question. An empiricist may stick firmly to the theory that the concept of a necessary being is absurd, and a metaphysician may persist in saying that the empiricist's denial involves an epistemological doctrine which is far from obvious, that all the criteria of cognitive validity are those which happen to have been elaborated in modern empirical science.

The myriad creatures in the world are born from Something, and Something from Nothing.
Lao Tzu, tr. D. C. Lau

The empiricist can go further. He can state that the very use of the concept of existence in the absolute sense is impermissible and that existence is a no less unintelligible idea than 'nothing'. When saying that an object exists we always mean that it belongs to a class of objects, or simply that it displays well-defined properties; we have no access to existence in the metaphysicians' sense, as opposed to 'nothing'. We can safely translate all the sentences in which the expression 'exists' or its negation appears into a language wherein the 'is' may be used only as a copula and then we get rid of all the seeming metaphysical mysteries; it is not the case that a horse has the property of existence, as opposed to Pegasus who has the property of non-existence: both statements are absurd unless they mean respectively 'horses (as defined by a set of properties) appear in experience', 'winged horses do not appear in experience'. Therefore not only assertions concerning a necessary being but sentences like 'something exists' or 'horses exist' are done away with.

This is, of course, a possible philosophical option: a radical phenomenalism coming very close to the ontological nihilism of Buddhist sages. If an empiricist is right in thus pushing his premise to the end – and I believe he is – then the concepts of existence and of nothingness, being on the same level of unintelligibility, are indeed removed from the field of our legitimate curiosity. If, on the other hand, we do admit the legitimacy of those concepts there is nothing to shield us from the formidable question of Leibniz: why does something exist rather than nothing? Once we admit this and face up to it, the necessary Being, Anselm's God whose non-existence is unthinkable, emerges as an intellectual compulsion. Again, the God thus forced upon our mind appears merely as a biblical '*sum qui sum*', not as the Christian Judge and Benefactor, yet this God is not a *figmentum rationis* either.

Once more, we face two irreconcilable options: either the standpoint of the radical phenomenalist, an ontological nihilism banning the very idea of existence from the society of intelligible entities *or* the admission that the question about existence leads to necessary existence. In the philosophical *instrumentarium* there are no commonly acceptable 'higher' principles to settle the clash between these options (except for spurious appeals to moral considerations, etc.). In the phenomenalist's eyes the metaphysician is powerless to 'prove' his point; in the metaphysician's view the very concept of 'proof', thus restricted, involves a philosophical option which he has no reason to take up. Both are right in the sense that both take a logically arbitrary decision, except that the phenomenalist is usually more reluctant to admit this.

CHAPTER 3

God of Mystics.
Eros in Religion

The words 'mystical' and 'mysticism' are widely used for various unconnected purposes. Some of them we may safely discard; we do not need to bother about the vaguely disparaging or downright sloppy ways the word 'mystical' is frequently used in order to say that something is incomprehensible or mysterious or strange or absurd or simply religious. Still, even when a more precise sense is intended, it has no commonly accepted limits, and in this it is not unlike all other religious and philosophical terms. In a broad sense the adjective 'mystical' denotes any experience people interpret as bringing them into direct contact with a non-human spiritual reality, whether or not God's presence is believed to be involved. According to recent research the incidence of this kind of experience is surprisingly high among people of various professions, creeds and levels of education. In a more restricted sense an experience is mystical if the person undergoing it feels himself to be in direct contact with God (no matter whether God is clearly and vividly experienced as a personal presence, or rather as the undefinable spiritual foundation of all being). This contact is usually – at least among Christian and Islamic mystics – permeated by the most intense effect of love, and associated either with a strong desire to achieve a perfect union with Him, to dissolve one's own personality in the boundless ocean of the Divine, or with the feeling that one has temporarily achieved this union. 'Mysticism' may refer to the entire area covered by this kind of experience, or to its literary expression, or else simply to a doctrine – whether or not personally tested – which implies that such an experience is both possible and genuine, not only in a psychological sense but in the sense that it really is what it claims to be.

Speaking of mystical life is bound to be even more awkward than speaking of God in speculative terms, and most of the great mystics repeatedly stressed the desperate inadequacy of the language they had at their disposal when trying to describe what they had lived through in their acts of union. They admittedly spoke of the Unspeakable; often they recommended silence as the best way of approaching God, and they violated their recommendation by the very fact of uttering it.

The experience of mystical union is a rare phenomenon, but still it may be said that it makes up the core of religious life. However unusual and however inadequately conveyed to us in writing, it is the only direct and, in the mystic's mind, absolutely irresistible experience of the Eternal and Infinite as such. In this respect it may be contrasted with limited forms of religious experience like the feeling of God listening to, or responding to, one's prayer, like encounters with non-human intelligences, angels or devils, or like the mere sense of the divine presence. In the mystical union alone God, instead of being simply conceived of in speculative terms as an eternal, infinite and living ground of being, is known, or rather felt as such in direct 'touch'. This experience, though impossible to convey to others in its original quality, is decisive in keeping mankind's religious legacy alive; it is at the source of the great religions and it is reflected in most important literary documents of religious history.

The very expression 'experience of the Eternal and Infinite' indicates the fundamental impossibility of adequately describing the mystical union: how, indeed, can the Eternal and Infinite be 'given' originally in acts which involve

---

And the soul sees, tastes and experiences that God is closer
to it than it is itself, that it is more God than itself and that
it possesses Him, yet not as a thing and not as it possesses
itself, but more than anything and more than itself. And it
conforms itself to this light so that its joy, its life, its will,
its love and its seeing are more in Him than in itself.

Benoit de Canfeld

---

no abstract notions? This experience is 'direct' – as if it were the sensory perception, touching or tasting, as opposed to the conceptual grasping, of the divine – and yet it is not sensory at all: it might be, but need not be, associated with, or preceded by, visions and other sensory perceptions, but the great mystics have never attached much importance to those secondary phenomena, or have even dismissed them as obstacles rather than aids to the proper acts of unifying love. More often than not they have described the 'experimental', immediate character of those acts by all sorts of negative expressions. The soul in the state of union is void both of images and of abstract concepts; it does not think of God and it does not try to grasp Him in intellectual categories, an endeavour which is in any case both useless and beyond human possibilities. No mystic has tried to 'prove' God's existence: to him, this would be like trying to prove that honey is sweet or perhaps that water is wet.

No unprejudiced reader fails to receive an impression of extraordinary intensity and authenticity in perusing the great mystical texts which various civilizations and various religious traditions have bequeathed us. Neither can he fail to perceive, behind the cultural and psychological variety, the astonishing persistence of certain basic themes, which suggests that we have here to do with a rare human experience which is nevertheless as universal as love and fear. The mystics, though their language is lyrical rather than speculative, of course look for instruments of expression in their own religious and literary traditions. But what they have in common is extensive enough to make us think that there may be an immutable core in religious life. The Eastern tradition certainly tends to stress more strongly the process whereby the soul is melted or dissolved in the boundless sea of the Absolute to the point where nothing recognizably personal is left. In Western mysticism the themes of annihilation, total passivity and deification are not lacking, to be sure, yet whenever they have carried the unequivocal idea of a soul vanishing without trace in the abyss of Godhead, they occur among people who crossed the limits of established Christian tradition; some of these were officially condemned by the Roman Church, some have remained in a limbo of lost souls whom no Christian Church is ready to adopt.

The little space within the heart is as great as this vast universe. The heavens and the earth are there, and the sun, and the moon, and the stars; fire and lightning and winds are there; and all that now is and all that is not; for the whole universe is in Him and He dwells within our heart . . . The Spirit who is in the body does not grow old and does not die, and no one can ever kill the Spirit who is everlasting. This is the real castle of Brahman wherein dwells all the love of the universe. It is Atman, pure Spirit, beyond sorrow, old age, and death; beyond evil and hunger and thirst. It is Atman whose love is Truth, whose thoughts are Truth.

From: Chandogya Upanishad, *tr. J. Mascaró*

There were at least three reasons, theological, institutional and moral, why the literary or philosophical expression of mysticism met with obstacles – greater in some historical circumstances than in others – when it sought a recognized abode in established Churches. In the teachings of Christianity, as in all monotheist creeds, the infinite gap between the Creator and the creatures has always been crucial; to be accepted by, or united with, God could not abolish the fundamental distinction and indeed one could not approach God without admitting this distinction, not just as an ontological fact but as a moral and emotional attitude as well. The path to God is through humility, repentance, recognition of one's own sinfulness and impotence, in the awareness of an endless distance between oneself and the divine perfection – a distance that can be bridged by love yet never cancelled. To speak of equality, let alone of identity, between finite corruptible human souls and the immutable perfection of the Absolute was bound to seem blasphemous, the expression of an infinite hubris. To say, as Eckhart did, that we are transformed totally in God without any distinction being left, that God has given man everything He has given to His son, that all creatures are pure nothingness in a literal, not a metaphorical sense, could hardly fit in with time-honoured Christian teaching.

The love of God in man is God.
Pedro Ruiz de Alcaraz (16th cent.)

Christian mystics, with a few marginal exceptions, have never made claims to a union with, or an ontological conversion into, God as a result of human efforts or as a well-deserved reward for a man's merits in piety and contemplation. The union was not something to be expected, let alone deserved; it was an extraordinary gift of grace and one could contribute to it only by doing everything possible to suppress one's own will, to reduce the soul to a state of perfect passivity through which God might act. Yet the very claim that such a passivity is attainable as the result of a soul's self-destructive effort hardly differs from the idea of self-deification, since absolute passivity is nothing else than conversion into God; if the former can conceivably be reached by the exercise of contemplation, so can the latter. To be capable of achieving the state in which 'acts of will' – in the mystics' words – have been utterly swept away amounts to their replacement by God's will and thus to the loss of distinction between the human and the divine.

Certainly, the renunciation of one's own will has been a standard tenet of Christian moral teaching and perhaps nobody insisted on it more emphatically than St Augustine; a man doing his own will resembles the devil, he said. Indeed, in Christian, Islamic and Judaic terms, to follow one's own rather than God's will is not just a sin but the sin *par excellence*, the original source of all evil, the disobedience which caused the fall of both men and angels. Yet to abandon one's own will in an act of perfect obedience to God's orders is not the same as to destroy the ontological status of human personality, as many mystics conceived of their experience. In acts of voluntary submission to divine guidance, the will, and thus the integrality of the person, is neither annihilated nor replaced by God, and the abyss between the Creator and the creature, far from being closed, becomes only the more dramatically apparent.

Before I was I, I had been God in God, therefore I can be again once I am dead to myself.

Angelus Silesius

This is the main theological reason for the ambiguous position of mysticism in monotheistic creeds. The institutional reason is no less patent. The charismatic concept of the Church implies that it is the irreplaceable mediator between God and His people, and this is expressed particularly in the interpretation of the sacraments: acts performed by persons within the Church's order and supposed to involve the divine presence and to convey the force of grace. Yet a mystic does not need human intermediaries, his communication with the Lord is direct and therefore he may imagine – as many did – that he is free to dispense with the aid of ministers. For a radical mystic who believes that the only proper way to God is to search for Him in one's own heart and to 'taste' Him in unmediated encounter, priests and indeed the entire ecclesiastical organism are a matter of indifference, or must even be regarded as a hindrance to real contact. The mystic sees and feels God in any stone or any drop of water, and thus does not need a special piece of consecrated bread to gain access to Him. Enjoying divine love as a mode of his own existence, he has no reason to request forgiveness within the institutional framework of confession. He has a spontaneously disparaging attitude to the entire liturgical and sacramental side of religious life. In

---

Were your heart right, then all created things would be mirrors of life and books of holy teaching. No created thing is so small and worthless as not to bring before men's eyes the goodness of their God. If you were good and pure within, you would see all things clear, nothing between, and you would understand them all; and a pure heart sees right inside – to heaven and hell.

Thomas à Kempis, tr. anon.

---

short, a radical mystic, by the very act of his union with God, and without necessarily saying so, makes the legitimacy of, and the need for, a church doubtful at best, if not downright harmful. Radical mystics are potential, if not actual, rebels within an ecclesiastical community. They profess an allegiance to God alone and, of course, if they think that there is a clash between God's direct orders and the Church's requirements, they cannot hesitate about which loyalty comes first. Ecclesiastical suspicion of mysticism is quite understandable: anybody, after all, a lunatic, a power-greedy maniac, a soul possessed by demons, may claim to be anointed of God; it is an important task of the Church to prevent the faithful from falling prey to self-appointed friends of God and false prophets, and to define criteria whereby genuine piety can be distinguished from delusions, charlatanism and diabolical temptations.

Take away the point and there is no line. Take away God and there is no creature. Yet not the converse holds.

Valentin Weigel

The third, the moral reason why ecclesiastical institutions were suspicious of mystical religiosity, was by no means without foundation. Those Christians who claimed privileged access to direct channels of communication with God easily persuaded themselves that they were not bound by the usual norms of conduct. They might have appealed, as some did, to St Paul's assurance that they were under grace and no longer under the law, and have interpreted this grace as freedom, granted to the elect, from traditional moral rules.

There were in mystical religiosity other components which might have – but by no means must have – led to similar antinomian conclusions. An incurable ambiguity seems to have persisted in the mystical approach to the created world, and one finds, in some mystical writings, an oscillation between two extremes, both apparently emerging from the same experience and neither of them compatible with the Christian Churches' teaching. The mystic wants to know and to desire nothing but God, any attachment to, or interest in, the creatures being in his eyes an idolatry and a barrier on his road to perfection. In traditional Christian teaching the pious were expected to love God as the unique absolute good without however denying a relative or subordinated value to finite goals if properly placed in the hierarchy of goods; in the created world there are things and qualities which may pass for autonomous though not absolute values (*finis ultimus secundum quid*) and there are others which, without having any intrinsic value in themselves, are instrumental in bringing about or in gaining autotelic goods (so, for instance, human life is good in itself but not the absolute good and thus it might be sacrificed for the sake of God; whereas food has no autonomous value but it is good insofar as it sustains life, etc.). Not so for a radical mystic. God being not only the highest but the only proper good, the creatures have not even a derivative or instrumental goodness; a radical contemplative's life is an effort to abolish entirely any mental, cognitive, moral, or aesthetic involvement in the world of finite things – including ultimately himself – and to focus exclusively on God in the hope of being eventually absorbed by Him. Seeing in the corruptible universe nothing more than a mass of obstacles barring spiritual progress, he is easily tempted by a kind of Manichean world view wherein everything material is of satanic origin, the devil is literally 'the prince of this world' and spiritual liberation consists in liberation from all ties with matter – nature, body, physical processes.

In the knowledge of good and evil man does not understand himself in the reality of the destiny appointed in his origin, but rather in his own possibilities, his possibility of being good or evil. He knows himself now as something apart from God, outside God, and this means that he now knows only himself and no longer knows God at all; for he can know God only if he knows only God. The knowledge of good and evil is therefore separation from God. Only against God can man know good and evil.

Dietrich Bonhoeffer (1930), tr. N. H. Smith

This attitude can, however, take two opposite directions: the theocratic-ascetic or the antinomian-anarchist (or, occasionally, a strange combination of both). The mystic of Manichean inclinations might say: the body, being intrinsically and incurably evil, has to be kept under the strongest possible control and fettered as tightly as possible; in other words our earthly life ought to be regulated by an exacting discipline lest the unholy desires of our wretched body spoil the purity of the spirit imprisoned in it. So reasoned the Cathars: Manichean condemnation of matter led to the ascetic withdrawal from an impure world. Yet from the same principle one might arrive at quite opposite practical conclusions, following the 'devil-made-me-do-it' logic: since my body is helplessly in the clutches of the demon and the soul is my only concern, my proper course is not to worry at all about the body's doings and to leave it to its own perdition, after having separated my spiritual ego from its ties with matter. Thus a contemplative might well remain in this state of union with God, undisturbed by his body, which is meanwhile free to perform, for instance, various dirty sexual acts with other bodies, preferably ones also abandoned by their spiritually advanced owners. This was roughly the logic of Miguel de Molinos' quietist piety and one of the reasons for its condemnation by the Church.

And yet, instead of suggesting scorn for the corrupted world, a mystical approach might easily have induced a contemplative soul to discern the divine *pleroma* in the whole variety of creatures, and thus to be enraptured with them, rather than repelled. To such a contemplative the universe appears not as veiled revelation of a great craftsman whose hand may dimly be perceived behind, or rather may logically be inferred from, his products, but as the direct presence of the unspeakable One. The oscillation between contempt for the world (because it is not God) and its deification, its admiring acceptance (because it cannot but be God in action) produces this ineluctable ambiguity which is manifested in mystical experience more obviously than in other forms of worship, and yet is rooted in the very idea, basic to all forms of monotheistic worship, of the One begetting the Many.

Knowledge is good. Thus, the authorities teach that when one knows creatures as they are in themselves, that is 'twilight knowledge', in which creation is perceived by clearly distinguished ideas; but when creatures are known in God, that is 'daybreak knowledge', in which creatures are perceived without distinctions, all ideas being rejected, all comparisons done away with in that One that God himself is.

Meister Eckhart, tr. R. B. Blakney

Before we turn our attention to this crucial question, wherein almost every fundamental concern of man's religious history is concentrated, let us see what moral and philosophical consequences may be drawn from the 'pantheist' (as opposed to the Manichean) variant of mystical experience, provision being made for the fact that these two apparently incompatible world views do not necessarily appear separately, in hostile confrontation, but frequently make up two poles of the same experience (some mystical writers indeed to not seem to be aware of the tension this polarity generates in the minds of their readers). I have put the term 'pantheist' in inverted commas. In fact a world entirely pervaded by the undifferentiated Godhead which unveils itself fully in every grain of sand and in every leaf of grass, does not need to be, though it may be, pantheistic in the proper sense of that word. To a pantheist the creatures are not only to be seen as God's signs, as God expanding into, or disclosing Himself to, our minds: there is a mutual and necessary dependence at stake, a substantial link binding God to the universe, and therefore it is as improper to speak of a purposeless world which indifferently follows physical laws, as it is to imagine God 'beyond', a fully self-satisfied entity who might have manufactured, for reasons known to Him alone, finite things, but otherwise has been left unaffected by His productive activity. It is better to explain the way in which a pantheist depicts the world in terms of mutual, necessary dependence between the Creator and the creatures than to use more familiar metaphors about God moving and guiding the universe 'from within', about His being 'inside' the world and imposing on it an 'immanent' purposeful order; such expressions suggest a topological relationship, which is usually not what had been intended by philosophers or religious thinkers to whom the label 'pantheism' is applicable. It is true that both theological and epistemological discussions are almost unavoidably crippled by the inherent inability (pointed out by Bergson) of the language to rid itself of spatial representations and patterns in describing non-spatial relations and qualities and that the expressions borrowed from those models – including 'in', 'to', 'inside', 'outside', 'beyond', 'immanent', 'transcendent' – sound clumsy or even pointless when God/world or subject/object oppositions are referred to. A complete escape from spatial figures is clearly impracticable, yet one might achieve a partial escape. This is the reason why we should try to avoid the overworked vocabulary of 'immanentism', the most commonly employed in the context of pantheistic beliefs.

God who is the totality of all these must needs include all things in his infinite being, while he himself cannot be included by any other thing. If there is anything outside him, he is then not the totality of all things, nor does he contain all things.

St Irenaeus, tr. H. Bettenson

Of these I shall refer only to the spiritual variant. Naturalistic pantheism or the attempt to shift on to Nature certain divine properties – purpose-oriented change, providential wisdom, creativity – is sometimes an effort to bring God closer to human experience, even at the price of depriving Him of recognizable personal traits; and sometimes it hardly differs, save in phraseology, from an outright atheism (to say that the world is God amounts to saying that there is no God, as Hobbes aptly remarked). It may be associated with a kind of quasi-mystical worship of Nature, of its admirable sagacity (as witness Giordano Bruno or Campanella); this however is only a pale copy of mysticism proper, and, historically, naturalistic pantheism appears undoubtedly as a cultural vestibule of the mature Enlightenment, happily satisfied in its godlessness. However important in the vicissitudes of European civilization, it is beyond the scope of the present discussion.

Spiritualist pantheism, on the other hand, includes both the belief that God manifested in His creativity is God proper (as against a view of the universe as a coded message from which His remote presence may be deduced) and that reality is of a spiritual nature. Being indivisible, He cannot be, of course, the raw stuff things have been made of; His unspoiled plenitude is to be found in every fragment of the world and thus whatever is, is divine.

No thing can partake in God's essence and yet this essence has to be even in the devil.

Angelus Silesius

This vision of the world which is not infrequently to be found or hinted at in mystical literature, gave rise to a number of consequences which established Christianity, not surprisingly, found theologically paradoxical or morally risky. Apart from their obviously inadmissible tendency, mentioned above, to blur the borderline between God and his creatures (especially his subjects endowed with reason), the pantheists' readiness to see God's face in every atom of dust led them, naturally enough, to neglect, to disregard, or to be incapable of admitting, the reality of Evil.

I have already pointed out some of the tremendous problems provoked by the presence of Evil in a God-governed universe. The pantheists' dismissive attitude made these problems even worse and less manageable. In the established tradition of monotheism moral evil, although of course not caused by God, and lacking an ontological foundation, was real and at least partially unredeemable. The being could not but be good, yet the ill will of men and demons, unavoidably enacting their freedom or self-determination, was a genuine energy directly challenging God's order and plans. But there is no place for such an energy within the pantheists' vision. They are strongly tempted to believe, without necessarily saying so in so many words, that whatever occurs is divinely inspired and must be part of the providential project. On this assumption the very distinction between Good and Evil is difficult to define, and we tend to be confident that all our deeds, however viciously motivated, not only generate good 'objectively' according to God's grandiose design, but actually *are* good; the whole of moral education is thereby undermined or simply made pointless.

Thus the mystical-pantheist adoration of the all-pervading spirit of God could yield the same moral carelessness as did the opposite doctrine which included the Manichean scorn of matter; it could justify a kind of moral anarchism ('don't worry, whatever you do, you are God's worker').

It might be argued that in both cases a convenient moral permissiveness was drawn from either Manichean or pantheist premises only by marginal groups or individuals and that no such intentions are attributable to any of the really important philosophers, thinkers or mystics. Yet the question of what place, if any, can be given to Evil, and of how it can be explained, was nonetheless alarming, even if it emerged within profoundly inspired, panoramic visions of universal history: in Johannes Scotus Erigena, in Hegel, in Teilhard de Chardin.

There has been in Christianity a recurrent refusal to admit that the ultimate salvation of the world would not be total, that some evil was unredeemable and that cosmic history included wasted elements, not to be absorbed in the final act of redemption. The painful mystery of the eternal damnation of both demons and men was the focus of conflict. Time and again there have been people who felt unable to reconcile the idea of an infinitely good and merciful God with the image of never-expiring infernal fire. At the Constantinopolitan Council in 543, Origen and the Jerusalem monks who had been spreading his doctrine were condemned for asserting that 'the torments of demons and of impious men are temporal' and that 'Lord Christ will be in the future crucified for the sake of demons'. The Armenian Church was condemned in 1341 by Benedict XII for stating that Jesus's passion 'had entirely destroyed hell'. Erigena believed in the all-embracing salvation of the universe (though he might have been inconsistent on this point, as he was on many others). So apparently did Teilhard de Chardin, even though he did not say so explicitly. Papini wrote a book to prove that the devil would be reintegrated into the Kingdom.

The issue is by no means trivial, or insignificant in religious terms. Indeed, what is at stake is the meaning of the ultimate unity of reality; and this issue has been the main dividing line between Far Eastern wisdom and the Middle Eastern and European religions of revelation.

Another peril inherent in mystical experience, in terms of institutional religious education, has been the mystics' claim to participate in the divine eternal Now, to enjoy the fullness of timelessness in which all distinction between past and future has been done away with. In such a state of immobile *praesens* there is no memory of the has-been and no anticipation of the would-be, indeed the very difference has been abrogated and lost meaning. Consequently, the mystic leaves behind a number of those virtues and feelings which have been deemed indispensable equipment of Christian advancement: both those related to the past – regrets, repentance, awareness of guilt – and those which look forward, like the fear of divine punishment, scruples, hope, deliberations over actions to be taken. While the mystic revels in communication with God, the all-engulfing Now is not disturbed by the flow of time. In short, all the criteria to which our daily life is subject fall away, deprived of sense. The radical mystic is beyond good and evil in the same sense as God is.

In him who depends (on others), there is wavering. In him who is independent, there is no wavering. Where there is no wavering, there is tranquillity. Where there is tranquillity, there is no passionate delight. Where there is no passionate delight, there is no coming and going (in rebirth). Where there is no coming and going (in rebirth), there is no falling from one state to another. Where there is no falling from one state to another, there is no 'here', no 'beyond', no 'here-and-yonder'. That is the end of woe.

Attributed to Buddha, tr. F. L. Woodward

This ability to leave aside the rules of everyday Christian moral teaching which include the differentiation and the hierarchy of virtues and vices is reinforced by the mystic's effort to purge his consciousness of all selfish motives, including the desire for his own salvation. This supreme renunciation, which is to be found in the texts of various mystics including those of impeccable Catholic orthodoxy, like St Theresa of Avila, is a natural concomitant of the theocentric attitude: we ought to love God for His own sake and not because He promised us the bliss of eternity; He is the end in itself and not a means to serve human needs, even the need of salvation; we must accept and admire His will unconditionally and in advance even if it includes our damnation (*resignatio ad infernum*). To get rid of all thoughts and desires related to oneself appears to many mystics an integral part of proper worship; only pure, perfectly disinterested love deserves the name of love as distinct from self-interest.

In view of this rapid survey of the risks that mystical religiosity carried (from the standpoint of an ecclesiastical body) it might be expected that the better a church is organized and the more strictly submitted to explicit rules of conduct, the less it is likely to tolerate this kind of worship within its institutional framework. This is not, however, the case. The Christian Church glorifies itself with an impressive gallery of great mystics it rightly considers the brightest stars in its spiritual firmament, starting with St Paul himself, the most venerated patron of Christian contemplatives; the history of Christianity would seem to us not only impoverished but unthinkable without Pseudo-Dionysius, St Bernard, Tauler, St Catherine of Siena, St John of the Cross, St Theresa, Bérulle and many others.

The soul which is a virgin and receives nothing save God can become God-pregnant as often as it wants.

Angelus Silesius

Many theological and moral criteria were invoked in deciding whether or not a mystical God-seeker could find his or her place, sometimes a very prominent one, in the life of the Church. They may be briefly summed up as follows. First, the ontological distinction between God and the soul has to be left intact and any suggestion that the mystical union involves a total annihilation of personality and absolute passivity is to be avoided; some recognized Christian mystics arguably failed to meet this criterion, which in some historical circumstances was more rigorously observed than in others. Secondly, a mystic may never use contemplation as a pretext for disregarding the traditional rules of obedience, let alone the common moral duties; he is supervised by his confessor like anybody else and even if he claims to have been given orders by God which run counter to the standard of obedience, it is the latter which has to prevail. In particular, he is not entitled to make statements relevant to dogmatic issues and to pretend to a special source of wisdom; if he utters a judgement unacceptable to the Church, he has, upon the latter's verdict, to retract it without hesitation (this is what happened to Fénélon). Thirdly, a mystic's experience, if genuine, strengthens his common virtues of humility, charity, chastity; it proves to be a diabolic temptation, rather than God's gift, if it breeds hubris, indifference to others, or irregularities of conduct.

It was therefore understandable that the phenomenon of mysticism was much more tolerable to the Church if it was confined to the closed world of monasteries where the rules of ecclesiastical discipline were more easily enforceable and where it was relatively simple to control undesirable contagion. When it arose among laymen or even among secular priests, mysticism easily provoked suspicion, and if it took a collective shape it was almost invariably condemned. Sometimes it then developed into more or less short-lived sectarian movements. After the Reformation the Roman Church appeared to be much more capable of assimilating mystical phenomena within its forms of religiosity than the great Protestant bodies. This was not only because it could provide them a relatively safe enclave in contemplative orders, which the Protestants could not do, but because of its much larger tolerance of the variety of religious life. In spite of the importance which mystical sources had both in the intellectual formation of Luther himself and in fertilizing the cultural soil for the Reformation in France, Protestant churches, with their stress on uniformity of worship and their democratic constitutional principles, proved to be naturally reluctant to absorb special forms of religiosity accessible only to a spiritual elite; in the hard-line Protestant literature, from Jurieu to Niebuhr, mysticism has been repeatedly denounced as a dangerous illusion of irresponsible *Schwärmer* or a relic of pagan gnosticism. Mystics who emerged within or on the margin of the Protestant movement, from its earliest phase in the 1520s in German countries and in the Netherlands, either abandoned the new Churches or were abandoned by them, occasionally forming tiny sects or going back to the Roman Church. Northern mystics, the spiritual heirs of Meister Eckhart, continued his metaphysical and speculative orientation in a neo-platonic style, whereas the rhetoric of Catholic contemplatives in Spain and France was more

---

He who loves God cannot endeavour that God should love him in return.

Spinoza

---

lyrical and more emotional; they were less concerned with finding a consistent expression for the unspeakable Oneness and more with reaching the inexhaustible source of love. By the end of the seventeenth century Catholic mystical piety had almost broken down, largely as a result of the severe condemnation of Quietism by the Church.

The historical vicissitudes of mysticism are, however, not central to this discussion. The point is rather to explain why this peculiar 'experimental' approach to God is of paramount importance in trying to grasp the very nature of the Sacred in cognitive terms.

The paradoxical character of mystical life has been just

pointed out: it is supposed to be an experience of Infinitude and thus, in terms of rationalist strictures, a square circle; it is indeed hard to conceive how Infinitude, instead of emerging in our mind as a conceptual abstraction, could be directly given as such, i.e., could make up the actual content of an experience; such claims sound like saying that one can see, touch or taste the very quality of something infinite. Yet this claim is at the core of mystical writings and makes them essentially untranslatable into the language of sensory experience, except through admittedly clumsy and inadequate metaphors. Mystics are well aware, and stress this repeatedly, that their words, though perfectly intelligible to kindred souls, are bound to appear inept or self-contradictory to others. Some say they found God hidden in their souls and waiting, as it were, till they discovered Him, others prefer to speak of God coming to them and taking possession of their soul. To some this happens in sudden unexpected moments of illumination, others go through long periods of agony, lost in a 'spiritual desert', in despair and in the certainty of being condemned. All gain an unshakeable and direct, non-intellectual knowledge, immune to criticism, of what the metaphysicians in their idiom hold to be the fundamental tenets of a religious world picture: God's necessity and the contingency of the world. Both tenets, no doubt, are philosophical translations of ideas which the symbols of faith express differently: that God is an omnipotent Being who created all things visible and invisible, and that the world as a whole and each thing separately depends totally on His will.

These tenets, which theologians claim to be able to establish as a result of speculative reasoning, are a part of the mystic's direct experience. What a philosopher laboriously tries to expound in abstract and often abstruse categories, a mystic sees. Occasionally, he describes his experience of the contingency of creatures by saying that the world is an illusion. This idea, so boldly expressed, is, of

When a free mind is really disinterested, God is compelled
to come into it; and if it could get along without
contingent forms, it would then have all the properties of
God himself . . . Unmovable disinterest brings man into
his closest resemblance to God. It gives God his status as
God . . . The disinterested person, however, wants
nothing, and neither has he anything of which he would be
rid. Therefore he has no prayer, or he prays only to be
uniform with God . . . When the soul achieves this, it loses
its identity, it absorbs God and is reduced to nothing, as
the dawn at the rising of the sun.

Meister Eckhart, tr. R. B. Blakney

course, inadmissible to Judaic, Christian or Islamic faith, all
of which firmly assert the reality of whatever God brought
into existence (otherwise Jesus himself would be no more
than a phantom), whereas it is traditionally assimilated
within the Buddhist and Hindu legacy.

Perhaps – this is no more than a speculative suggestion –

Unmoving – One – swifter than thought,
The gods could not seize hold of It as It sped before them:
Standing, It overtakes all others as they run;
In It the wind incites activity.

It moves. It moves not.
It is far, yet It is near:
It is within the whole universe,
And yet It is without it.

Those who see all beings in the Self,
And the Self in all beings
Will never shrink from It.

From: Iśa Upanishad, *tr. R. C. Zaehner*

the chasm between these two streams of religious tradition is less gaping than it might appear. On the one hand there is beyond doubt a special kind of experience which is best expressed by saying that the world around us is 'unreal' or 'illusory'. This experience is fairly frequent, by no means confined to mystics, and noᴛ necessarily interpreted by people in religious terms. We may set aside the question whether and to what extent it is similar to, or identical with, the feeling of 'unreality' which seems to be a common aspect of certain pathological states of mind. Whatever its origin, it is hard to put the experience so described into a verbal form claiming to be a metaphysical proposition. To state that a certain object is 'merely an illusion' is, first of all, intelligible only by the criterion of social consensus. A hallucinatory or delirious perception may be labelled as such only in contrast with other perceptions that pass for 'normal'; consequently the meaning of such a qualification, when it is extended to include the world as a whole, is never clear, no matter how intense or authentic the feeling behind it. And that one person's perception is an illusion other people cannot prove without ultimately appealing to the verdict of the majority. Still, sayings like 'the world is but an illusion' may make sense if they mean either that all things are inherently impermanent, fragile, corruptible or, less trivially, that to be in time is not in the proper sense to be. This last meaning is perhaps the basic component of the 'world-is-a-dream' insight. The importance of this insight consists in that it is something that can be both directly experienced, apparently without the mediation of abstract philosophical concepts and also explained, at least tentatively, in metaphysical terms. We may observe both sides of this intuition mixed up or perhaps fused into a whole in the famous eleventh book of St Augustine's *Confessions*, certainly one of the most daring attempts to cope with the issue, and in Angelus Silesius' collection of epigrams *Cherubinischer Wandersman*. In mystical writings similar reflections are fairly common.

The main idea boils down to this: whatever belongs to the past or to the future by definition does not exist, except in memory or in anticipation, i.e., subjectively; meanwhile the present, on closer inspection, shrinks to an evasive and unattainable point which by definition disappears as soon as we try to capture it. Thus, whatever is 'in' time, never 'is'; it may be spoken of as something that was or that will be, yet such sayings make sense only when a perceiving subject is implied. Things which have no memory owe their continuous identity only to our minds, whereas in themselves they have no past or future and thus no identity at all. We endow the world of corruptible things with duration and thereby with subsistence, yet in this very act of mentally producing it we realize our own lack of identity, except as it is supplied by memory. This amounts to stating that whatever is, is timeless. And so, we go back to the great initiators of European metaphysics, Parmenides and Heraclitus, who from opposite sides set in motion this dizzy whirligig of concepts: what changes, is not; what is, is beyond time; if there is nothing beyond time, nothing exists.

For existing is not one thing and always existing another.

Plotinus, tr. A. H. Armstrong

This equation stating that to be is to be beyond time yielded the natural conclusion that whatever is, is unlike material objects, and so is a mind: yet a mind thus obtained through reflection has to be radically different from what we know introspectively, i.e., from a 'moving' thought, feeling and perception. It was less natural to conclude from the same equation, and without further premises, that only one existent or mind is conceivable, and still less that this mind is a person; yet the eventual merging of the neo-platonic Being with the Judaic and Christian God seems to us understandable if we consider the necessity (historical, not logical, to be sure) of translating the original myth into the Greek philosophical idiom and of reforging the Bible into a metaphysical story.

Rabbi Abba spoke: What did the Israelites mean by saying: 'Is the Lord among us, or not?' (*ayin*, nothing; Exod. 17:7 . . . The explanation is, as Rabbi Simeon has made it, that the Israelites wished to ascertain whether the manifestation of the Divine which they had been given was of the Ancient One, the All-hidden One, the Transcendent, who, being above comprehension, is designated *ayin* (nothing), or whether of the 'Small Countenance', the Immanent, which is designated YHVH. Therefore for the word *lo* (not) we have the word *ayin* (nothing).

One may ask, why then were the Israelites chastised? The reason is they made distinction between these two aspects in God, and 'tried the Lord' (ibid.), saying to themselves: We shall pray in one way, if it is the One, and in another way if it is the Other.

From: the book of Zohar, *tr. Gershom Sholem*

This merging was clearly a condition of the success of Christianity and thus of the entire intellectual history of Europe as we know it, but it has never been quite satisfactory, and this for more than one reason.

It has been pointed out that it was a very difficult, if not conceptually impracticable task, to combine smoothly the notion of a perfectly self-contained impassible *actus purus*, of a Being that alone *is* in the proper sense, with all the qualities normally attributed to a person. The image of a tender and merciful Father implies properties which were hardly in keeping with this metaphysical entity. How can the Absolute be subject to affections? How can He have a perfect knowledge of individuals, including His human children, given that He *is* whatever He knows and that, consequently, both people and things have to have, in addition to their empirical existence, a kind of ideal model in the divine mind, God being still perfectly simple and uncompounded? These puzzles were to plague the late scholastics, and if philosophers wanted to remain faithful to the traditional teaching and to believe in a God who is simultaneously Plotinus' One, the Old Testament's angry Leader and Jesus's loving Father, they were bound to confess their helplessness; no intellectual effort could pierce the ultimate mystery. To admit that was simply to accept the incurable frailty of human reason and the priority of faith. Yet the formidable question had to be answered: are we to admit not only that God's essence is beyond the reach of our intellectual capacity – which no Christian philosopher has hesitated to say – but moreover that once we try to speak of Him in philosophical terms we cannot escape contradiction, which means not only that our reason is defeated in its attempts to understand God but that its fundamental principle is simply violated, faith being both *supra* and *contra Rationem*?

There was a great variety of standpoints among those Christian writers who were ready to admit not just a difference between the capacities of Reason and the truth of Faith, and not only a need to keep them separate, but their outright incompatibility. Both the philosophical and the cultural significance of this clash varied in time. The defiant anti-intellectualism of some of St Paul's letters and of Tertullian's magnificent *'certum quia impossibbile'* has never entirely died away in Christian civilization, yet its meaning depended on a given historical setting. In late antiquity it expressed uncompromising rupture with the values and norms of an unredeemed society, the tough self-confidence and self-identity of revolutionaries who did not belong to, and refused to negotiate with, the pagan world and were building within it an alien enclave. The gradual encroachment of Christianity upon this society and its eventual dominance had to be paid for by the infection of Christianity with some of the society's standards and by the assimilation of its rationalist weapons. Yet in the new phase of conflict between the anti-intellectualism of old and the attempt to provide Christian teaching with a rational foundation, the roles of the protagonists were reversed. Starting with the late eleventh century, the anti-dialecticians who condemned secular knowledge were now speaking for a securely established Church, whereas their adversaries who displayed their logical skills in religious matters and could not suppress their curiosity in profane science, had become the spiritual spokesmen of a burgeoning urban civilization, one of those unavoidable by-products was the emancipation of the intellectual class. To be sure, Abelard's aggressive rationalism was an exception. Those who, more or less consciously, supplied a rationale for the independence of the profane arts tried to separate the matter of the arts from that of theology in such a way as to affirm that the two areas do not enter into any logical conflict, since their respective interests do not overlap. But this attitude was hard to uphold consistently; there were important questions which obviously fell into the field of competence of Reason, but which had already been decided by Revelation, like the beginning of the universe in time. The extravagant endeavour to affirm both the possibility of a clash between knowledge and revelation and their independent authority is known as the theory of double truth; some of its proponents among later Averroists maintained that one may believe simultaneously in conflicting truths (e.g., the world was created out of nothing, and the world has existed eternally) provided that one made a clear distinction between the two orders of cognition.

Thus the cultural function of the tendency to admit the contradiction between the revealed World and natural light depended on what value, if any, was attributed to the latter. Both the aggressive 'Tertullianism' of anti-dialecticians,

> Do not imagine that your own intelligence may rise to it,
> so that you may know God. Indeed, when God divinely
> enlightens you, no natural light is required to bring that
> about. This natural light must in fact be completely
> extinguished before God will shine in with his light . . .
>
> *Meister Eckhart, tr. R. B. Blakney*

which asserted this contradiction in order to defend faith
and the Church against the claims of 'human logic', and the
schizophrenic concept of double truth which used the
contradiction to defend the rights of the same logic were
short-lived phenomena in mediaeval Christianity. The
mainstream of those who sought to grant a cognitive and
institutional independence to secular learning devised
various criteria separating its scope of interest from
theology, while the latter's claims to supremacy found
eventually a well elaborated and precise expression in
Thomist doctrine. This stated unambiguously that the truth
of revelation and the achievements of natural reason, both
originating in the same divine source, could never contradict
each other. Therefore, if the latter affirms something
contrary to faith, it must have violated its own principles. So
theology, without pretending to replace or to make useless
natural knowledge, retained its right to supervise it, it having
been accepted that natural light enabled us to discover truth
in some matters which nevertheless had already been
decided by revelation. Thus the two areas overlap, yet on
many of the most important points we can gain insight into
truth only by faith (these points include not merely the
truth about the Trinity, the Incarnation and Redemption
but the question of the temporal beginning of the universe
as well).

The distinction was no doubt very fortunate in terms of
the Church's needs for self-definition in a world where

profane knowledge and profane values increasingly asserted their authority and self-reliance; yet the very assent to this duality – a hierarchical duality, to be sure, by no means an equality – risked encouraging the grievances of autonomous philosophical inquiry beyond the limits of safety. Aristotelianism, though apparently well-assimilated within the framework of Christian concepts and safeguarded against the exorbitant pretensions of a bolder and bolder Reason, would not fail to create the same peril it was supposed to stave off: it was to become an intellectual vehicle whereby Christianity slipped down the path towards secularity and thus toward oblivion.

Looked at from this perspective the Reformation was a violent attempt to restore the pristine purity of the Christian message and to cure it of contamination by profane values (at least these were its original intentions, although its long-term historic effects were to turn against these intentions, as has been the case with most of the great human ventures). In its early stages it returned to a primitive Christian consciousness based on a sturdy trust in divine promise and not bothered at all about what the wisdom of the schools might adjudge; it sneered at the subtleties of mundane dialectics and it made of philosophy a dirty word; it brought havoc into the German universities.

The curious fate of the never-ending faith-versus-reason debate in the centuries which followed the salutary shock of the Reformation (salutary for the Roman Church, that is) seems to bear out the common-sense truth that in an urban civilization where movement, change, development, and novelty pass for eminent values, no permanent and satisfactory covenant or armistice between the Sacred and the Profane is likely. By doing away with the Church's continuous tradition as a source of authority in interpreting the Scriptures, the Reformation, as it turned out and precisely in opposition to the wishes of its great initiators, promoted a more, rather than less extensive use of Reason in theological matters. The march of rationalism could not be stopped and it produced ideological rearrangements on both sides of the conflict between Enlightenment and Tradition. Scholastic methods of supporting religious truth with rational arguments were progressively losing credibility and efficacy, and although the masters of the mediaeval schools never stopped exercising their semantic and logical skills, they were soon to be regarded as uninteresting remnants of a past age, incapable of competing with, let alone of matching, new intellectual trends either of the empiricist or the rationalist kind, all of them contributing to the merciless corrosion of faith. Seventeenth- and eighteenth-century deists and adherents of 'natural religion' who cut away from the Christian legacy whatever they thought was rationally unprovable, clearly crossed the limits within which Christianity could remain recognizably itself; their successors were prompt to show that if we want to apply strictly the rigours of rationality to the prophetic books of old, the entire fabric of ancient wisdom would fall apart. The first generation of deists were people led to despair by the spectacle of a religious fanaticism, displayed by warring sects and factions, which the eruption of the Reformation had brought to life; their religious rationalism was at the service of tolerance and peace. Most of them certainly believed that the few basic religious tenets which really mattered – God's existence and providential rule of the world, the immortality of souls, Christian moral norms – could be well justified on rational grounds, whereas all the intricate and in fact unintelligible mysteries of trinitology or the theory of grace, all the dogmas and anti-dogmas which incite sectarian wars, killing and persecutions, have no meaning whatsoever and are beyond the legitimate interests of the human mind. The idea of rational religion did away with all the beliefs on which the distinction between various churches within Christianity – or even, in a more radical interpretation, the distinction between all the religions of the world – had been grounded. It took a long time before this instrument of tolerance would breed the intolerance of fanatical rationalism.

The same irenic results could have been obtained (not in reality, of course, but in the heaven of wishful thinking) and were repeatedly attempted by the opposite intellectual device: not by chopping religion down to its 'rationalizable' size and thus converting it into a second-rate knowledge, but, on the contrary, by following time-honoured tradition and declaring the entire body of beliefs to be founded on the divine authority alone. This was not enough, however, since each denomination made claims to the infallibility of its own interpretation of the Scriptures. Therefore, ecumenic proposals based on the idea of a religion which was a matter of faith or of 'sentiment' had to make all the conflicting interpretations irrelevant, purposeless or simply illicit. One possibility was to recommend that we confine our faith not only to what the Scriptures said but to the exact way in which they said it, and forbear to comment on them or venture into philosophical reconstruction; the assumption being made that in all matters which are really important and relevant to our salvation the Scriptures are clear and unequivocal enough. This was a frequent attitude of the followers of Erasmus, who preached religious peace.

Another way of achieving peace was, of course, an efficiently working intolerance. It was not a new contrivance, to be sure; yet the traditional defence of the Church's monopoly used to be grounded on its exclusive ownership of truth, whereas for some seventeenth-century advocates of intolerance the decisive reason was, on the contrary, that there is no truth in the normal sense in any Church or in any among the competing denominations. Hobbes and certain of the French libertines were of the opinion that it was the task of the state not to allow people to massacre each other because of different views on how the bread in the holy communion is transubstantiated into our Lord's flesh. An

absolute order and an obligatory state religion were pro-
posed as the best guarantee of peace, yet the main virtue of
this religion would be that it was the only one allowed, and
not that it was truer or more credible than its rivals.

However, seventeenth-century French libertinism (and I
refer to the *libertinage érudit* and not to moral libertinism,
the latter having been in some cases connected to the former
but by no means necessarily or universally so) encompasses
a range of attitudes about the matters we are discussing. It
was typical of this *Weltanschauung* to separate religious
from empirical questions, and to profess loyalty to the
Christian tradition as conceived in fideistic terms. There is
no doubt that some libertines, though entirely contemptuous of sterile – in their view – theological disputes,
genuinely believed in the fundamental tenets of the Christian creed, i.e., in God and eternal life, while dismissing
attempts to make those tenets credible on rational grounds,
whether scholastic, Aristotelian or Cartesian. This was, we
may presume, the attitude of Gassendi, of La Mothe le
Vayer, perhaps even of Naudé. What was genuine in their
beliefs had no denominational flavour, though, since all
theological quarrels which divided Christianity were in their
eyes uninteresting at best, and usually meaningless and
empty. If they professed their allegiance to the Catholic,
rather than to any other, Christian Church, this was a civil,
as opposed to a religious commitment; they believed it
proper to observe the customs and the tradition of the
country they happened to live in: collective forms of
religious life deserved respect for political and social, not for
dogmatic reasons (among earlier humanists, Justus Lipsius,
the great editor and reviver of Stoicism, changed his
denomination five times, depending on the country he lived
in; his main philosophical work is entitled *De Constantia*.)
There were others, however, to whom such fideistic declara-
tions were probably no more than a protective mask to
conceal incredulity, and sometimes it is not easy to decide

which category a given person belonged to. Pierre Bayle, who enjoyed the reputation of a thorough sceptic hiding behind the phraseology of sentimental religiosity, was (as it appears from the studies of Elisabeth Labrousse) a sincere believer; but the weighty influence he exerted on the Enlightenment was that of a sceptic and destroyer of faith; his readers shrugged off his protestations of piety as one more example of a tactic lavishly employed by cautious atheists.

Yet it should be noted that the fideistic approach to the Christian creed, combined with scientific phenomenalism and empiricism, was shared by people like Mersenne who by no standards could be listed among the libertines and whose piety was never called in doubt.

As long as open godlessness was risky it was quite common for doubters occasionally to pledge their religious fidelity as a matter of irrational faith; they could be distinguished from serious believers by their style and distribution of emphasis, yet in some cases there was doubt which was which. Philosophers who, like Pietro Pomponazzi, David Hume and many in between, collected arguments against the immortality of the soul and yet professed to accept it as a revealed truth in spite of these arguments, could hardly be given credence. On the other hand the return to the concept of a Faith boldly defying the claims of Reason was frequently a very serious attempt to defend Christianity in a cultural predicament where the rationalist critique appeared to have produced some irreversible and irrefutable results. This was essentially the attitude of Pascal in facing the invasion of Cartesianism (a somewhat crude assessment, to be corrected later).

In this respect we are still heirs to the conflict which has been going on since the late Middle Ages, and which became increasingly conspicuous in the seventeenth century, when the rules of the modern scientific spirit were codified in the works of Bacon, Galileo, Descartes, Locke and Gassendi, among others. Christian intellectuals were ever more aware of the simple fact that in terms of the discipline governing empirical investigations and of the expanding use of mathematical methods, the legitimacy of the traditional metaphysical approach was increasingiy open to question. The position of natural theology was becoming obviously shaky and insecure in confrontation with a concept of Reason monopolistically defined by the norms of scientific procedures. One may speak of the 'escape into irrationality', yet the expression carries a strong and contestable value judgement. In stigmatizing beliefs or kinds of behaviour as 'irrational' we necessarily imply a well-defined concept of *Ratio* and this concept itself is always open to doubt: can we produce any compelling grounds for a definition of *Ratio* without employing criteria whose validity depends on the previous acceptance of this very concept? And so, let us talk not of an 'escape into irrationality', but of an expanding awareness of the irreducibly different ways in which religious beliefs are validated in contrast to scientific propositions, of the incommensurable meanings of 'validity' in those respective areas.

Kant himself may be located in this perspective. He tried to demolish the seeming certitude of the old natural theology and yet to rescue it by rebuilding it on entirely new principles. In arguing that belief in God's existence and in eternal life are indeed justifiable within the scope of practical reason, he did not convert those beliefs into moral or technical norms; his assumption was only that some normative ideas can be validated independently of theoretical reason and that, being valid, they necessarily imply God and immortality as truths in the common, and not pragmatic, sense of the word. Thus he managed not to deviate from his dogged rationalism.

In the Catholic world it was the Modernist crisis at the end of the last and beginning of this century which drastically revealed the clash between the pretensions of natural theology and the victorious march of scientism (scientism, far from being a logical conclusion inferrable from the body of scientific knowledge, is an ideology stating that cognitive value is defined by the proper application of scientific methods). The Modernists (Alfred Loisy, Edouard Le Roy) shared a phenomenalist approach to science and a symbolic interpretation of religious faith. Science, they argued, does not deliver to us truth as we usually understand it; it is a convenient schematization of empirical data into theoretical constructions whose value is manipulative and predictive, rather than cognitive, if the latter term suggests a description of the world as it 'really' is. On the other hand religious truth can never properly be crammed into intellectual forms: its basic insights are variously embodied in symbols subject to change, none of them representing an ultimate version and none being free from contingent, historical means of expression; the Scriptures are a historical document and so are Church dogmas which are bound to evolve along with the development of civilization. And the only reliable access to religious truth is by way of a private experience which cannot be satisfactorily rendered in intersubjective discourse.

The separation of revelation from science is now complete: the latter has no means to issue verdicts about the Divine and it does not deal with reality at all, its meaning being utilitarian, rather than cognitive; whereas in acts of faith we gain an intuition into another, divine reality, yet this intuition can be conveyed only in culturally relative symbols. It is a misuse of science, the Modernists argued, to make religious or anti-religious judgements in its name and it is a misuse of religion to define rules in, or to make pronouncements upon, matters pertaining either to scientific inquiry or to secular life. Science and religion differ in almost everything: in their objects, in the way they gain their respective knowledge, in the very meaning of the truths they claim (neither of these, in fact, constituting the truth in the everyday and Aristotelian sense).

And so, the Modernists hoped to resolve conflicts between profane knowledge and revelation by defining for each a different epistemological foundation. The proposal was obviously unacceptable to the Church and for more than one reason: on the Modernist postulate Christian dogmas were deprived of their immutable veracity and had to be taken as provisional historical expressions of revelation; in religious matters the main source of insight was supposed to be a kind of mystical contact with the divine reality, and as a result the very function of the Church either became unclear or was reduced to its historically immanent tasks; and the Church, thus robbed of its everlasting charismatic legitimacy, was told in addition that it should not interfere at all in secular life, let alone in scientific controversies. The enormous scale of the Church's battle against Modernist error in the first two decades of this century proved the vigour of the heresy. And indeed, though seemingly victorious (in the sense that it effectively banned the condemned formula from official theology) the Church sustained immense losses. By refusing to take up the challenge, by displaying its inability to assimilate modernity, it was step by step losing control over cultural life and repelling the educated classes. The problems the Modernists had raised could not be, as would become evident, cancelled by anathemas and by the repetition of the optimistic assurances of Thomism about the consonance of secular and religious knowledge.

And indeed the Modernist contagion was not cured, since it was not some freak heretical idea on the part of a few intellectuals but the expression of a deep rift in a civilization that seemed to be built on intellectual principles and on values which were increasingly incapable of a harmonious co-existence with its religious heritage; neither could the awareness of the collision be switched off, nor the quest for new solutions bridled.

The paradox of the conflict we have been witnessing throughout this century consists in this: the chief motive which stimulated various mediaeval attempts to separate the Profane from the Sacred was the defence of the former, the desire to liberate science from theology, to release state institutions and public life from ecclesiastical supervision. But seemingly analogous trends in modern times usually pursue the opposite end: to shield the Sacred from the rapacity of the Profane, to uphold the legitimacy of faith in its encounter with rationalist doctrines, to assert the rights of religious life within a culture which has canonized its own secularity. The social meaning of the separation is thus entirely different, yet its epistemological foundation is often the same. Apart from those who – like the Modernist thinkers just mentioned – drew a line of demarcation between two realms in the hope of their future non-interference, our *saeculum illuminatum et illuminans* has begotten more searching and rebellious spirits who realized that the clash was real and not merely the result of conceptual misunderstanding or logical sloppiness. They opted for God against, and not in addition to, the world. They did not try to appease secular Reason by finding a modest enclave sheltered from its voracity and by begging for permission to survive, they attacked its intrinsic inability to cope with worries which are bound to be crucial in our life – unless they are concealed *mala fide* – and they expressed the revolt of faith, well aware of its status as a foreign body, indeed a fearful disease, in this civilization. The Russian Jew, Leon Shestov, and the Spaniard, Miguel de Unamuno, belong to this category; their way had been paved by the great nineteenth-century foes of Enlightenment – Kierkegaard, Dostoyevski, Nietzsche – people who refused to negotiate with a self-satisfied rationalism and progress, who refused to patch up the antagonism.

All these men were to become prophets of our time, a time in which our everyday world picture is ambiguously clouded by the never fading awareness of both the blessings and the horrors of scientific progress, and moreover a time

in which the established churches find it increasingly hard to
devise a language reaching the souls of contemporary men,
and often, to their doom, attribute such failure to their being
not 'progressive' enough, i.e., insufficiently submissive to
the requirements of modernity, too 'religious'. In the very
title of his best known book, *Athens and Jerusalem*,
Shestov embraced Tertullian's intransigence; and he took
the side of biblical myth against the self-decreed supremacy
of analytical Reason: the tree of knowledge and the tree of life
do not grow side by side in friendly harmony; eating from the
former led to death, to eat from the latter is a hope which
Reason can never legitimize, indeed Reason is bound to
regard this hope as a threat.

Both Shestov and Unamuno, not unlike Kierkegaard
before them, started with the experience which, they
believed, stubbornly and eternally resisted absorption by
any rational framework of knowledge; my self-awareness of
being myself. Their common approach may be perhaps
restated as follows: to say 'I am I' is not a tautology; neither
is it an example of the universal Aristotelian principle of
identity; nor is it equivalent to the statement 'John is John'
uttered by another person. The natural mechanism of
Reason is to subsume everything individual and unique
under abstract concepts; but 'I' may not be thus subsumed.
'I' refuse to conceive myself as a particular case of a concept
and refuse to be so conceived by others. Whoever starts with
this act of self-assertion sees immediately that it is absurd to
say that there are two or more 'I's and yet, in terms of
analytical Reason, it is absurd to deny that there are many
'I's. Consequently, we face two incompatible absurdities,
one of which we have to accept; insofar as Reason mono-
polizes the power of judging what is or is not absurd, we
admit that we follow what, in St Paul's words, the world has
to see as folly. The implacable objectivity of Reason forbids
me ever even to name, properly speaking, what I know
– and what everybody else knows, for that matter – to be

the indestructible realm of my ultimate concern: my existence, my salvation, God, moral choice. 'I' am not a thing, nor is God; to neither of us can Reason assign an ontological status, and therefore Reason is compelled, by its very rules, to reduce us to something we radically are not: to objects. In trying to grasp myself and God I put myself inevitably into a position of anti-rational revolt, since Reason is necessarily the destroyer both of myself and of God, both being beyond the limits of its capacities for assimilation. And life confronts us with choices which are inescapable and in which we may expect no help from the resources at the disposal of Reason, from scientific knowledge, from technical skills. In short, to take religious issues seriously is not just to by-pass the competencies of Reason but positively to opt against it, as Reason asserts itself only by asserting its indisputable monopoly in deciding what is or is not knowledge, what we may or may not legitimately think, which choices are real and which imaginary.

(God's) concept is not like that of man under which the individual is subsumed as a thing which cannot be absorbed by the concept. His concept comprises everything, and in another sense He has no concept. God does not help Himself by an abbreviation, He comprehends (*comprehendit*) reality itself, all the individuals; for Him the individual is not subsumed under the concept.

Søren Kierkegaard, tr. W. Lowrie

Have we reverted, ascending blindly on a historical 'spiral', to the Christian wisdom of old which had defined itself by baldly anathematizing secularity, modernity, science? It would be an exaggeration to say so. There are various trends, vying with each other, in today's religious disarray. A dwindling band of buoyant theologians still hope that they may endear themselves to the Enlightenment and

raise their speculations to the status of a respectable branch
of science; there are many who still look to appease secular
civilization by delineating the respective estates of *sacrum*
and *profanum* and by trying to talk the two powers into
pledging a mutual treaty of non-interference; there is a
theocratic tendency, not very vigorous in Christianity, to be
sure, yet fairly robust in the Muslim world; and there is the
contrary (or seemingly contrary) fashion for reducing
religious tradition to one or another political ideology. An
acute feeling of conflict is present everywhere; which among
these attempts at readjustment will prove victorious or at
least strongest in the near future nobody can predict; we
may, however, have an opinion as to which, if they achieved
dominance, would be the most likely to destroy the religious
legacy of mankind.

The mystical tradition as a whole cannot be clearly located
on the map of these controversies. Most mystics have never
bothered to phrase the question of Faith and Reason in
categories which were familiar to philosophers. They have in
common a strong negative conviction that profane Reason
and 'human' logic could be of no help in anything that really
matters in human life, i.e., union with God and knowledge of
Him (if there is for them any sense at all in this distinction;
usually there is not). Some mystics are content with a few
contemptuous phrases about the vanity of secular science,
others stress the implacable hostility between Faith and
Reason; still others (Eckhart and Cusanus for instance)
speak of a higher cognitive faculty, Reason or Intellect,
which affords us insight into the divine infinity and which is
guided by principles of its own, principles which, on closer
inspection, turn out to be opposed to, rather than to
supplement, the rules of common logic, whether or not this
contradiction is explicitly stated.

If we turn to mystical texts written by more philosophi-
cally oriented authors, we notice that they were invariably
aware of the fact that knowledge about God, whether gained

in contemplation or through speculative effort, lies beyond the power of language and appears paradoxical. Pseudo-Dionysius, in his treatise on the divine names, says that God has no name and that one has an equal right either to apply or to refuse to Him any name: since our thinking is incapable of grasping the divine unity, no assertion and no negation may, properly speaking, be uttered about God. He recommends therefore that we ought to forbear from saying or thinking of God anything save what He wanted to reveal us in the Scriptures.

Interpretation finds its limit where language stops. It is consummated in silence. And yet this limit is there only through language.

Karl Jaspers

Similar ideas are to be found in most neo-platonic philosophers, Christian or not. Plotinus' immortal work is full of restrictions about the incurable poverty and inadequacy of the language he is using. Eckhart was not afraid of recognizing the self-contradictory character of theological discourse and Cusanus tried to work out a new logic of infinity where the principle of contradiction was replaced by the principle of *coincidentia oppositorum*, convergence of contrary qualities when they reach their limit-values.

The main source of contradiction appears to have been always the same, and it was identified by all the speculative mystics: the Oneness of Being confronted with a created world consisting of many objects. Nobody trying to conceive the question failed to be struck by a sense of logical impossibility: the rationalists converted this into a quasionto-logical argument for God's non-existence (I cannot think of God without falling into contradiction, consequently I cannot think of God without denying His existence); for neo-platonic and mystical theologians the same impossibility

proved that our logic had a limited validity and was helpless
in dealing with God.

Every created thing desires to be natural again, to be what
it was before the creation . . . The elements were created
out of nothing and their desire is to be nothing again.

Paracelsus

The question has been broached already, yet one particular aspect of it still needs to be mentioned. In terms of those
traditions which explicitly admit the concept of the Absolute, the world manifests God and conceals Him at the same
time: by the very fact of being a non-absolute, it leads us to
God as its necessary condition and by the same fact it bars
the road to Him, since our thinking and perceiving are
imprisoned within it and the Absolute is beyond the reach
both of our senses and of our concepts. Once it has been
assumed that Being is One, the world of many, the variety of
things and souls becomes inconceivable. We are tempted to
escape the contradiction by denying not God's existence but
the existence of the world: many is One. This theme recurs
time and again in the mystical literature of various civilizations (Rudolf Otto in his classic work on Eastern and
Western mysticism points out a striking similarity between
the speculation of Meister Eckhart on the one side and the
writings of Sankara and other Oriental mystics on the
other). It appears that all things and all souls in their 'real'
existence are God and that our return to God is the
restoration of our 'genuine' mode of being, of what we truly
are; individuality is seen, so to speak, as a pathology of being,
an ontological curse, as Schopenhauer would have had it.
The same insight may be expressed variously: 'all is one',
'the Kingdom of Heaven is in you', or (Angelus Silesius) 'the
abyss of my soul shrieking invokes God's abyss; say, which
one is deeper?'

This self-contradictory idea that 'many is One' is by no means an invention of speculative minds; that the whole and the part are identical is, as Durkheim observed, tacitly or explicitly assumed in all religions. In his view people expressed and asserted in this concept of all-embracing unity the cohesion of the social body; far from simply displaying (as Levy-Bruhl had once suggested) the lack of logical skills and the mental helplessness of savage people, the idea of mystical participation was the way in which the authority and the supremacy of the social 'Whole' was recorded and consolidated in the minds of individuals. This explanation does not make clear why people all over the world needed this kind of fantastic projection of the societal 'totality' and could not be satisfied with simpler means of strengthening their tribal solidarity. Nor does it explain how they were able to produce, for the purpose, an imaginary universe bearing no resemblance to the empirically known world and in no way suggested by experience. These doubts, however, are beyond the limits of this discussion. What I am getting at is merely that the most elaborate ontological constructions of speculative mystics are rooted in an elementary and universal experience of the Sacred.

Those who tried to convert this experience into a conceptually consistent 'system' were fated to reveal its inconsistency; what believers had naturally accepted in the language of myths became problematical and even inconceivable after such a transmutation. By being remade as theology, they myth exposed itself to the rigours of 'normal' logic and fell prey to the inquisitiveness of sceptics. Not only Christianity but, for a limited period, Islam has gone through this ordeal.

Yet mystics knew that they were challenging common logic and impertinently refused to surrender. Their claim, again, is to have *experienced* this identity of the part and the Whole; they live in it, rather than know it as it has been codified in myths and laboriously explained in metaphysical

At first there was only darkness wrapped in darkness.
   All this was only unillumined water.
That One which came to be, enclosed in nothing,
   arose at last, born of the power of heat.
In the beginning desire descended on it –
   that was the primal seed, born of the mind.
The sages who have searched their hearts with wisdom
   know that which is, is kin to that which is not . . .
But after all who knows, and who can say
   whence it all came, and how creation happened?
The gods themselves are later than creation,
   so who knows truly whence it has arisen?
Whence all creation had its origin,
   he, whether he fashioned it or whether he did not
he, who surveys it all from highest heaven,
   he knows – or maybe even he does not know.

From: Rig Veda, *tr. A. L. Basham*

systems; they neither need to produce evidence for this experience nor are they bothered by its logical incoherence when it is verbally expressed. And Western mystics, at least, are satisfied that the 'metaphysical curse' is remediable without personal consciousness being destroyed in the process. It is neither the case, they feel, that an individual soul, in order to survive, has to carry forever, even in heaven, the burden of its separation from the source of being, nor that ultimate salvation consists in being utterly dissolved in the impersonal sea of spirit. They believe they have really lived 'temporarily in eternity'; their experience has proved to them that it is possible to achieve identity with God without forfeiting one's own personal life; the laws governing the world of finite things cease to operate in the realm of the divine.

Still, when he realizes the glaring insufficiency of the

linguistic instruments at his disposal, the radical mystic frequently feels compelled to say that in communicating with God one ought to keep silent and to strive to empty one's mind not only of words but of concepts and images as well. This is the virtue of *oratio mentalis* as opposed to vocal prayers. Here, certainly, is the supreme form of spiritual life and a stage one can arrive at only after the long preparation through the usual mental exercises; once a mystic has reached it, however, he can and ought to dispose of all subsidiary means of approaching God. But what is suitable to the most advanced souls may not be attempted by beginners. And, he often adds, when we speak of God we should remember that our words can never properly grasp the reality they pretend to depict. Therefore the meaning of our discourse is pragmatic, rather than cognitive: theological formulae do not so much convey a knowledge of God as they exhort us to adore and to obey Him in humility and in awareness of our own ignorance.

Thus we notice a strange convergence between the cognitive attitude of a radical mystic and that of a radical sceptic. By virtue of a *coincidentia oppositorum* the mystic and the sceptic turn out to be twin brothers in epistemology. In keeping with their premises, they ought perhaps to remain silent rather than try to expound their ideas, and indeed this is what they not infrequently recommend. Yet in both cases, as I have already remarked, this recommendation appears to be fraught with pragmatic antinomy: it is being violated by the very fact of being uttered. The antinomy is perhaps avoidable if we restrict the meaning of both mystical and sceptical silence. A sceptic does not say that he should be silent altogether; nor does he argue that no knowledge is possible. He rather believes that what we say in everyday language has a practical, rather than cognitive value and this assumption is perfectly sufficient in normal communication between people; we must not endow our words with the additional virtue of being able to depict the world as it truly is and we ought to abstain from making epistemological comments about the cognitive sense and the criteria of validity, including presumably sceptical comments. A sceptic is thus inconsistent not by being a sceptic but by saying he is; he is not inconsistent when he simply talks but he is suspected of inconsistency if he discusses, justifies or explains his sceptical philosophy. A mystic is in a very similar position. He may well believe that it is useful, indeed necessary, to speak of God, but only on condition that the meaning of our talk is practical and that we do not pretend really to know what God is. What we know is not expressible in language: a sceptic *qua* sceptic may go that far.

And both for a sceptic and for a mystic there is one remaining means of escape when they try, in defiance of their own norms, to explain the epistemological basis of their refusal to ascribe to their words a cognitive value (an explanation apparently impossible without the admission of something whose inadmissibility makes up the content of their explanation). They may say, with Wittgenstein, in whom perhaps the sceptic and the mystic reached agreement, that their explanation is indeed meaningless and that therefore it may and ought to be thrown away like a ladder one has already climbed. Mystical teaching on the stages of spiritual advancement includes a similar injunction. And Cusanus' concept of *docta ignorantia* combines both senses, mystical and sceptical.

One may argue that one crucial epistemological distinction between a sceptic and a mystic still remains, for all the similarities: the latter has gained a perfect certainty, the former has none. Yet it is not necessarily so. A sceptic does not at all need to live in a psychological state of uncertainty: epistemologically he is an ascetic, rather than a rope-walker. What he knows suffices for him to live and to communicate with others and, if he is consistent, he simply does not bother about philosophy. Nor does a mystic.

I am not arguing that scepticism and mysticism are the same thing, or that they are analogous in every respect. My point is, first, that the epistemological approach is similar in both and, secondly, that it is not inconsistent or monstrous to be a sceptic and a mystic at the same time.

And yet those who amalgamated a mystical *élan* with metaphysical curiosity fed on neo-platonic tradition could not find comfort in the inexpressible security of a personal encounter with God. They did not want to escape from the tormenting riddle which Proclus and Plotinus had tried to cope with: why had One begotten many? What might have prompted the self-contained Absolute, having no desires and no needs, to give birth to the variety of finite, corruptible beings breeding evil and misery?

The answer which tempted some Christian Platonists was that God indeed had needed the creature He had brought to life. This implies, of course, that God is not the absolute being. He is not at the beginning what He will be at the end of the great journey. He begets the world in order to ripen in its body, as it were; he has to make something alien to Himself and to see Himself in the mirror of finite minds and when He reabsorbs again His alienated products He grows richer; the magnificent and terrifying history of the world is God's own history, perhaps God's cosmic Golgotha, a precondition of His final glory.

God cannot be called 'omnipotent' without the existence of subjects over which he may exercise his power; and therefore in order that God may be displayed as 'omnipotent' it is essential that everything should subsist.

Origen, tr. H. Bettenson

In this highly unorthodox account the mystery of man and mystery of God are blended: they have, as it were, a common

itinerary and a common destiny, they need each other in the
voyage towards the ultimate reconciliation which can be
achieved only as the result of a split in Being and its
subsequent healing. Thus the concept of *felix culpa* has
been raised to an ontological dimension, as though the
original sin, i.e., a break with God, had been committed first
by God who tore Himself asunder in emanating the universe.

Various elements of this story, told with various degrees of
consistency, may be found at the peripheries of Christian
theology, among writers either heretical or of dubious
orthodoxy; Erigena, Meister Eckhart, Boehme, Angelus
Silesius might be mentioned in this context. The general
framework of the story can arguably be traced back to
various cosmogonic myths in India and Iran. And its
substance was taken up in the grandiose panorama of
Hegel's historical ontology: the drama of an Absolute Being
which, not satisfied with its empty self-identity, alienates
itself and, through the struggles and tragedies of human
history, matures to a perfect self-consciousness, re-assimi-
lates its products and eventually abolishes the distinction of
subject and object without destroying the wealth of forms
which emerged on the way.

This version of the story may be labelled dynamic
pantheism, its assumption being not only that a *vinculum
substantiale* joins God with the world but in addition that
this link is formed and manifested in purposeful historical
evolution. It endows with meaning both the act of Creation
which from the standpoint of established Christian theology is beyond understanding (the excess of divine goodness overflowing beyond itself) and also human history,
including its monstrous and its sublime aspects: history is
now seen in terms of both God's and man's growth. The
price to be paid for this gain in understanding is that it
leaves us with the image of a historical God, God-in-
process, and this appears at first glance entirely out of
keeping with Christian tradition.

Is this really so? Have we to do with two absolutely irreconcilable ideas: God-in-becoming versus God as an immobile Absolute? Perhaps the opposition is less radical than it seems. To be sure, the fact that some Christian thinkers were strongly tempted by neo-platonic theogony without considering themselves any less Christian is in itself not decisive, as they might have erred in failing to notice the incompatibility, and in most cases they were indeed castigated as heretics. Yet the incompatibility may be questioned on metaphysical grounds.

The historical God of neo-platonism seems un-Christian for three main reasons. First, this theology was usually associated with so-called 'emanationism', a doctrine implying that God had generated the world out of His own 'substance', rather than *ex nihilo* or *post nihilum*. Yet it is arguable that the difference is rather one of words than of content. Established Christian theology assumes that to be is to participate in the source of Being and that created things, whether bodies or spirits, though not parts of God, are of Him; their existence is contingent, yet not independent. Neither did the Platonists see the creatures as parts of God (in their terms this would be, if anything, even more nonsensical than in Christian theology, considering the stress they laid upon God's absolute unity). Nor did the Christian expression '*ex nihilo*' suggest that Nothingness was a stuff which God moulded things of: there was no stuff other than God Himself.

Since the one Infinite alone exists, necessarily there is nothing except it . . . The existence of all things is the existence of deity.

Zwingli

Secondly, the 'emanationist' concept implied a kind of ontic necessity in the process of gradual descent from the

One to matter, which seemed to run counter to God's free arbitrium. This question, which I have discussed earlier (chapter 1) was shown to yield to the argument that the distinction between being free and being necessary is inapplicable to God.

Thirdly – and this is the crucial point – the concept of a historical God seems to be self-contradictory from a Christian point of view, as the Absolute is by definition the ontic plenitude, lacking nothing, desiring nothing, impassible; nothing could conceivably be added to God and nothing could make Him more perfect than He is.

On this point, however, the Christian God has never been free of ambiguity; He is above all the God of love, and it takes two for love to exist: self-love is not love as we understand it. Hence it is hard to imagine a childless God without anyone to love, and it is natural to think of Him in terms of His encounter with man; in other words the believer tends to assume that God is what He is – a loving Father – only in an I-Thou relationship; or that He does indeed need His spiritual progeny.

Properly speaking, God in Himself is nothing. He is without will, effects, without time, place, person and names. He becomes something in creatures, so that only through them does he receive existence.

Sebastian Franck

To this one may reply that, according to Christian teaching, whatever God created in time (or rather 'with time') had existed in Him throughout His eternity, given God's timelessness and actuality. Yet such an explanation, instead of doing away with the ambiguity just mentioned, brings it more distinctly into relief. We can understand our existence as conscious subjects only in relation to time, and the divine eternal Now is beyond our normal experience of time. Hence in terms of this experience our strange metaphysical pre-existence in God's immutable womb is not only beyond the reach of our memory but does not fit in with our understanding of what it is to be human. This involves our sense of 'subjective' self-identity. To say 'you have lived in God for ever without knowing it' means simply 'you have existed for ever as a dead object'.

It is indeed unthinkable that anything could be 'added' to the immobile perfection of Spinoza's and of the Buddhists' Absolute, for it is quite indifferent to the fate, to the suffering and indeed to the very existence of wretched little creatures crying out from self-inflicted pain on the surface of a minuscule globe which drifts aimlessly through the void. Yet the Christian God, we are taught, is not indifferent to us; therefore it is unimaginable that our existence and destiny could not affect Him. Time and again the same incongruity looms up when the God of the Christian myth is confronted with the impassible *Esse* f metaphysicians. Neo-platonists needed a creative demiurge to mediate between the One and the world, and Christians elaborated the idea of the eternal Mediator and the doctrine of the Trinity; yet they have never given up the belief that God is both Father and the Absolute.

Something else is possible to us: in the awareness of the phenomenality (*Erscheinungshaftigkeit*) of everything we know, to realize the presence of the Wholly Other through which everything is and we are.

Karl Jaspers

The mystics claim to have overcome this incongruity; they are sure that they have experienced a God who is both. Nothing is easier than to dismiss their pretensions on the ground of their incoherence. The mystics shrug off such objections: they saw what they say and if what they saw, when put into words, appears logically unsound, they do not care; so much the worse for logic.

And so, two irreconcilable certitudes collide with each other: the certitude of philosophers resting on the criteria of coherence and the certitude of believers and mystics who participate in a myth or in the reality the myth refers to. And who is wise enough and impartial enough to decree imperiously which criteria ought to be given priority? And what might 'priority' and 'impartiality' mean when applied to this collision?

CHAPTER 4

The Sacred and Death

Above and beyond all anthropological inquiry into various beliefs in an after life and in the definitive victory over death, there are two non-empirical and non-historical questions: why have people, throughout known history, continued to cherish the hope of an endless existence and how has this hope been dependent on the worship of eternal reality?

The most obvious answer to the first question – that human idea of immortality results from the fear of death we apparently share with all animals – is the least credible. We do not know how the fear of death might produce the idea of the ultimate extinction and still less why it should instigate 'escape' into a belief in survival. If fear of death were a sufficient condition for the human concept of immortality, why have the sharks – who avoid death as much as we do – failed to create their own images of hell and heaven? Analogous questions may be asked, of course, about all qualities and experiences which are, or seem to be, rooted in universal patterns of life and which we endow with an additional meaning: if the entire erotic experience of mankind is to be explained in terms of the reproductive instinct, then what is wrong with the frogs, none of whom, to our knowledge, has ever written a *Tristan and Iseult* or a *Faust?* If religion is nothing but a device to compensate for suffering, why do not suffering mice build their temples and write their sacred books?

Such questions are by no means flimsy or extravagant. They bear on the very possibility of producing a satisfactory definition of the human race in terms of an evolutionary world view, and of explaining how the continuity of species has been broken by the emergence of man. After he heard Plato's definition of man as a two-legged, unfeathered animal, Diogenes of Synope, as Diogenes Laertius reports, brought a plucked rooster and said 'here is Plato's man'. The definitions of man in terms of morphological or physiological categories will always be targets for similar criticism, even if, unlike Plato's clumsy description, they are good enough to identify a specimen of the set. They must be suspected of constructing from our biological equipment a frame of reference by means of which to understand culture, and thus of implying that the entire cultural creativity of man – language, art, religion, science, technology and philosophy – may be sufficiently explained in terms of its instrumental function in serving the allegedly basic and unalterable needs we have in common with other species. Such theories, characteristic of the German naturalistic philosophy of culture, including Freud, are convenient and utterly unfalsi-

---

We have always been dying, and yet death has lost none of its freshness, its originality. Herein lies the secret of secrets.

Emile Cioran, tr. R. Howard

---

fiable, no matter whether they suggest that the ingenuity of the human species in contriving cultural tools to improve its living conditions proves its exceptional adaptability (this is how most philosophizing biologists and ethologists would have it) or, on the contrary, that in its very need to extend its natural mechanisms of self-defence and self-regulation by artificial cultural devices, our species displays its increasing biological impotence and that it is, so to speak, a degenerated offshoot of life, a cul-de-sac of evolution. Most philosophers who speculate on this subject tend not to subscribe to either of those doctrines. They believe instead that the artificial cultural environment which the human species has produced satisfies a number of specific needs which have become autonomous even if initially, at the very outset of humanity, culture was 'nothing more' than an assemblage of instruments serving our animal nature. This approach, even if it sounds more plausible than a purely functionalist one, is also unfalsifiable and cannot be substantiated by historical or anthropoligical material, however expanded; moreover, it leaves open the fundamental question of how this hypothetical autonomization of needs came about. What made human nature – i.e., the collection of genetically conveyed and invariable properties of the species – capable of producing new invariants in the form of cultural needs and how are those needs transmitted? How could it have happened that creatures who stood in need of eating, copulating and sheltering themselves against the elements, invented art and religion the better to satisfy those life requirements and then, for reasons unknown, started enjoying their inventions for their own sake? Why has no other species sharing the same needs produced anything comparable?

I do not intend to discuss these riddles, which provide the basic material of so-called philosophy of history. It suffices to point out that no empirically derived solution may be expected for them, and that any answer, functionalist or otherwise, is bound to remain speculative and governed by philosophical bias. We cannot analyse what human nature is, or what makes human history human, unless we have already determined at what point, in the evolution of species, our species begins, and how far back human history extends. The location of this point is a matter of choice.

From historical material we will never discover the absolute beginning of art, religion or logic. Jaspers rightly argues that we cannot coin even the concept of the universal history of man without placing ourselves, or at least trying to, beyond the universal history of man. Such attempts must probably be unsuccessful, insofar as we cannot mentally abandon the historical process we live in and through; yet they are not necessarily fruitless. But the act whereby we confer meaning upon the process as a whole must be understood as optional. Whatever this meaning might be – the endless progress of human self-creation, the decadence of life, the ultimate salvation or the ultimate disaster – it is not extracted from historical knowledge. Those who deliberately and openly locate this meaning outside the historical process, as the Christian philosophers used to do – St Augustine, Bossuet or, among our contemporaries, Daniélou and Maritain – are therefore more consistent. They admit, more or less explicitly, that a perspective from which the meaning of history can be seen must be able to embrace the entire process, including both the first fiat and (in Teilhard de Chardin's phrase) the final Omega point. Being by definition as inaccessible to us as a position from which one might see directly one's own face, this vantage point coincides with the divine eye; thus no glimpse from this all-encompassing perspective can be afforded to us directly, but only in the form of the revealed word of God. Consequently, revelation alone is the source of whatever knowledge we may hope to gather about the 'meaning of history' and indeed about the very validity of such a bizarre concept.

I tend to support this view. It seems that the question of meaning, here as in other areas of investigation, is void and illegitimate unless a channel is open to us whereby we can make contact with the eternal repository of meanings. To be sure, nothing prevents us from conferring, by a sheer act of will, upon the historical 'whole', a meaning which confirms what we feel we are, or might be, capable of; later on we can forget that free sense-generating decree and experience the world as if it were full of meaning in itself (a model example of 'alienation'). If we do not forget, we cannot cancel the difference between the pseudo-meaning which is only a projection of our desire and the meaning proper which implies that historical process has a 'destiny' or a 'calling'. Nor can the latter be discovered from within; it requires a reference to eternity and a belief that facts are more than they appear to be, that they are components of a purposeful order. If we are liable to such a belief, this is not because we perceive this order with our sober profane eyes, but because even those of us who either deliberately reject all religious beliefs or simply never pay attention to them nevertheless

---

The general character of the world is eternally chaos, not in the sense of absence of necessity, but in the sense of absence of order, or articulation, of form, of beauty, of wisdom . . .

Friedrich Nietzsche

---

harbour a hidden readiness or even a half-conscious compulsion to look for an order in the gigantic rubbish-heap we call the history of mankind. This compulsion may easily be dismissed by die-hard rationalists as the freak remnant of our mythological legacy or as a disease of language. And yet those who find themselves on the other side of the border-line drawn up by modern analytical philosophers (a line notoriously vague) are tempted to think that it reveals not only the contingent nature of mind but the mind's real link with the eternal ground of meaning, of which any description, however, is inescapably as relative and as bound to a particular civilization as language itself. In other words, they are drawn to think that the sheer fact of the widespread belief that man is intrinsically related to the Eternal and defined by this relationship bears out the content of this belief. No explanation of it which is unexplainable in terms of our physiological needs has been convincing, however many indirect links may have been invented in such explanations; neither for the very notion of Eternity nor for man's self-understanding by its mediation (Meister Eckhart's *aliquid increatum et increabile in anima*) is a biological root likely to be discovered.

Let us repeat: it is an ontological option to believe that the Eternal manifests its real presence by being throughout history a term of reference in human self-understanding. The contrary belief that a plausible explanation of the worship of eternal reality may be given in anthropological terms is an option as well. I have tried to explain why each of those options is self-supporting and why neither can be validated by the criteria of truth which the other employs.

It is against this background that the desire for immortality is to be seen. If indeed, as philosophers have repeatedly argued, the instinctive animal fear of being killed and the human horror of death have to be distinguished and the former does not offer a sufficient condition for the latter, the explanation may be sought in the ontological framework of culture, along the lines suggested by Heidegger's explorations. The inevitable extinction of the human person appears to us the ultimate defeat of being; unlike the

---

It is impossible that anything so natural, so necessary, and so universal as death, should ever have been designed by Providence as an evil to mankind.

Jonathan Swift

---

biological decomposition of the organism, it does not belong to the natural order of the cosmos. Indeed, it violates this order. Order, being empirically inaccessible, may be spoken of only when the *contingentia rerum* is related to a necessary and thus eternal reality.

Cinis aequat omnia. If personal life is doomed to irreversible destruction, so are all the fruits of human creativity, whether material or spiritual and it does not matter how long we, or our performances, might last. There is little difference between the works of Giovanni Papini's imaginary sculptor carving his statues in smoke for a few seconds' duration, and Michelangelo's 'immortal' marbles. And even if we do imagine that there is somewhere a god who turns the wheel of life, His presence is utterly indifferent to us: He may find an incomprehensible amusement in running and watching our destiny but in a while He will throw away the universe as a broken toy. Unamuno, in the first chapter of *The Tragic Sense of Life*, recalls a talk with a Spanish peasant to whom he suggested that perhaps there was God but no immortality; to which the peasant replied, 'So what is this God for?' This is indeed the spontaneous reaction of a believer: if nothing remains of human effort, if only God is real, and the world, after meeting its final fate, leaves its creator to the same void or plenitude He has always enjoyed, then truly it does not matter whether this hidden King exists at all. The point of this response is not that we selfishly crave a celestial reward or an infinite compensation for our finite misery, as the critics of religion have argued, but that if nothing endures save God, even God grows no better or richer as a result of human toil and suffering, and an endless emptiness is the last word of Being. If the course of the universe and of human affairs has no meaning related to eternity, it has no meaning at all.

Had not Infinite Goodness been the Law of Heaven, there had never been any other Being, but God.

Benjamin Whichcote

Therefore belief in God and belief in immortality are more intimately linked than their simple juxtaposition as separate 'statements' might suggest. They seem to be logically separable from each other, i.e., one may, without contradicting oneself, accept either belief and reject the other. Saducees, according to the testimony of Josephus Flavius, worshipped God and denied human immortality; so did their seventeenth-century spiritual descendant, the luckless Uriel da Costa who wrote a striking treatise on the subject, part of which survives; so do some people today. Conversely, there is nothing incoherent in believing in survival without believing in God. However, to believe in God and to accept the ultimate destruction of everything else is to make God signally 'useless' – not in terms of personal gratification but in the sense that God, from the believer's point of view, is the guarantor of meaning of the world, He is the purpose-giver, and apart from His relationship to the creatures we are hardly able to grasp His existence. The greatest mystics might have reached the level of a pure 'theocentric' attitude and worshipped God for God's sake alone, perfectly oblivious of anything that is not God; yet these very unusual feats of spirit can never set the standards of any socially established religious world outlook. On the other hand, to believe in personal immortality without God is to leave the question of meaning obscure: if there is no God and if the cosmos is indifferent to our life, what kind of strange natural law might guarantee us the blessing of immortality? Why should the universe be so constructed as to listen to our desires? And so, on both sides, the two notions seem psychologically and historically connected; the gift *par excellence* of religion – the world endowed with meaning – carries these two components interdependently.

If man did not die, if he lived forever, if thus there was no death, there would be no religion either.

Ludwig Feuerbach

In terms of this perennial function of the belief in immortality it is immaterial whether or not people have in addition, or think they have, or want to have, any empirical confirmation of survival. This is a matter of changing cultural conventions. In fact a civilization, like ours, where people are so eager to find experimental evidence of their hope for an after-life, far from displaying its laudable trust in 'scientific' methods, reveals only the uncertainty, the fragile position of the religious legacy. If, in many primitive cultures, people communicate with the spirits of the deceased, this is because they have some business to do, or because they have fallen prey to the nasty tricks of ghosts, and not because they seek an empirical confirmation of their faith. If events occur which to some people suggest evidence of reincarnation, they do not seem particularly important to, or zealously sought after by, the Hindus who do not need them at all to support their creed. Christianity has always been strongly mistrustful of all searchings after 'experimental' evidence of survival, whether in spiritualist séances or in other paranormal phenomena. The Roman Church in particular has been vehemently opposed to those endeavours; the Holy Office in 1917 formally forbade believers to take part in spiritualist sittings and Catholic literature on the subject clearly perceived the hand of the Devil in the performances of alleged ghosts (it is true that the Anglican Church was much more lenient in this respect, which might suggest an abatement of faith, rather than an invasion by empiricist attitudes). Christianity's doctrine of immortality has been based on God's promises and on Jesus Christ's resurrection, not on reliance on the conclusive value of experiments which may always be dismissed by rationalistically-minded critics, anyway, as they do not fit into the conceptual framework of contemporary science. Such investigations might have a value in themselves, and it is out of place to discuss here their persuasive force, but they cannot serve as a rational support for enfeebled religious faith; at best they might serve as its ersatz.

CHAPTER 5

To Speak of the Unspeakable: language and the Holy. The need for taboos

The question of meaning in religious language has emerged repeatedly in the foregoing remarks and it is now time to sum up and to defend the author's view on a few crucial points in this long-standing debate.

The main target of the empiricists' strictures has always been the failure of religious discourse to meet the usual standards which determine the admission of particular statements to the club of empirical utterances. No matter how rigidly or loosely those requirements have been defined and codified in the endless discussions about verifiability and falsifiability, the entire field of specifically religious language has invariably fallen prey to this criticism. It was not hard to show that, apart from purely historical statements which, for all the importance they might have in the body of beliefs (e.g., like 'a man called Jesus was crucified in Jerusalem in Pilate's time'), are not specifically religious, there was no way to translate particular beliefs into a language that would successfully stand the tests of 'empiricity'; neither are those beliefs analytic, setting aside the doubtful case of the ontological argument. Nothing that can be said about God, divine providence, the creation of the world, the meaning of human life, the purposeful order of things and the ultimate destiny of the universe, is either falsifiable or endowed with predictive power. I do not feel competent, nor do I need to intervene in the discussion about which is the best description of the rules of verifiability, as the general standard established by Hume and his faithful successors suffice to dismiss the claims of theological arguments to 'scientific' status.

It is true that such claims are still occasionally made, though they are by no means typical of contemporary Christian culture. They seem to me awkward and unconvincing. To take just one example which has the virtue of being widely known. The eminent theologian, John Hick, argues that God's existence can be known to us beyond any doubt in the after-life, thanks to Jesus Christ's revelation; such a verification cannot take place in earthly life, to be sure, but the point is that its very possibility is enough to show that the conflict between faith and atheism is not merely verbal and that the choice is not empty: the way in which we see the world and react to moral issues hinges on whether or not we believe in God's word *hic et nunc*. The argument hardly sounds persuasive. It is a common-sense truth that our religious beliefs are of importance to our moral life and our perception of events, yet this is irrelevant to the question of verifiability. And the possibility of a convincing proof in the after-life does not change the epistemological status of dogmas in our sublunar existence, provided that the form of such a verification is unimaginable. This is not a question of 'technical' versus 'physical' or 'logical' verifiability, but of the very sense of a verification procedure. Perhaps such a verification is possible without logical norms being violated in the process, but we lack arguments for or against this possibility. However it may be defined in the philosophy of science, verifiability ultimately refers to universally accessible acts of perceiving. The mystics are perfectly satisfied with the meaning of their experience and if everybody could share their feeling of illumination the discussion would be pointless and would have never arisen: God's existence would be both verifiable and actually verified. It is not, because only a few enjoy the mystical experience and no sceptical mind can be convinced of its authenticity in the sense to which mystics testify.

However, even if access to religious experience, mystical or otherwise, were common, and granted that a body of religious beliefs were, as a matter of fact, not questioned at all, it would still hold true that the validity of those beliefs was vindicated differently from the truth of empirical assertions. These two areas of our speaking, thinking, feeling and acting are fundamentally irreducible to the same store of experience.

This seems to be the crucial point in debates on the 'meaning of religious language'. The traditional arguments of empiricists are cogent if limited to the assertion 'religious beliefs are empirically empty'. The subsequent verdict (admittedly less vociferously repeated today than it used to be) 'therefore they are meaningless' is not credible at all. There are no transcendentally valid criteria of meaningfulness and no compelling reasons why the meaningful should be equated with the empirical, in the sense in which modern science understands this term. The edict establishing such an equivalence is far from being unquestionably admitted by empiricists other than die-hard Humeans, and this not only because of difficulties in devising a satisfactory definition of verifiability and analyticity, but simply because the ordinary meaning of meaning is by no means so rigidly restricted, nor are there any logical or epistemological grounds for such a mutilation. Theologians occasionally appeal to the loose rules suggested by the later Wittgenstein or by other pragmatically oriented philosophers to whom all expressions are meaningful insofar as the rules governing their use are established and agreed upon among users.

I am not attempting to fix upon any definition of meaning and I do not think it is important to this discussion. My point is negative: since we have no key to the treasury of transcendental rationality, all restrictions imposed on the implicit everyday criteria of meaning are royal commands issued *ex nihilo* by philosophers and carry no other legitimacy; they are enforceable only to the extent of the philosophers' sheer power. There is nothing wrong and nothing illogical in granting a meaning to anything that people say with a feeling of understanding and which other people receive with a similar feeling.

This is not to deny that the constitution of meaning in religious life is different in a number of aspects from the way meaning is formed and asserted both in everyday speech and in the language of empirical science (the latter being an extension and a codification of the former). The saying occasionally quoted by Christian theologians, 'God is an infinite circle of which the centre is everywhere and the circumference nowhere' is hardly a geometrical axiom and it would not be advisable to try to represent it in a drawing. We know what the metaphor means: the same as what theologians try to express by saying that God is a perfect unity, that He has no parts and no separable (*in re*) qualities, that none of His attributes are quantifiable, etc. We are more familiar with the latter modes of expression, therefore the bold 'geometrical' proposition might strike us as outrageously (or amusingly) absurd. Yet it is in no worse or better position than any properly theological statement, measured by the standards of science. Some mathematicians claim to be capable of visually imagining objects in four-dimensional space; are they not in a position similar to the mystics?

Several characteristics specific to religious, as against profane, discourse, need to be pointed out.

I started with the premise that the language of the Sacred is the language of worship and this means that its elements become meaningful in acts which believers interpret as communication with God: in ritual, in prayer, in mystical encounter. Religion is not a set of propositions deriving their sense from the criteria of reference or from their verifiability. Particular components of the language of the Sacred are bound to look incomprehensible or just plain nonsensical outside of the context of worship. In both everyday and

That which cannot be expressed by speech,
By which speech itself is uttered,
That is Brahman – know thou this –
Not that which is honoured here as such.

That which thinks not by the mind,
By which, they say, the mind is thought,
That is Brahman – know thou this –
Not that which is honoured here as such.

That which sees not by the eye,
By which the eyes have sight,
That is Brahman – know thou this –
Not that which is honoured here as such.

From: Kena Upanishad, *tr. R. C. Zaehner*

scientific discourse the acts of understanding and of believing are clearly separated, yet it is not so in the realm of the Sacred: the understanding of words and the feeling of participation in the reality they refer to merge into one. Jesus said: 'You do not believe because you are not sheep of my flock' (John 10:26). This amounts to saying that 'belonging to' precedes all proofs, which therefore are never proofs in the sense acceptable to a criminal court or to the editor of a scientific journal.

And in acts of worship, especially in ritual, religious symbols are not conventional signs or images; they work as real transmitters of an energy coming from another world. Therefore the meaning of words is constituted by reference to the entire space of the Sacred including both mythical reality and practical acts of worship. Almost any example taken from either an archaic or a universal religion will serve to illustrate this specific form of linguistic life. Evans-Pritchard, in analysing the religious language of an East

African tribe, points out that in this language the copula 'is' has a meaning different from the one it bears in everyday use; the confusion of two languages, in his view, led to Lévy-Bruhl's false theory of pre-logical mentality. One may say, in this religious language, that rain is God or that a bird is spirit, yet never that God is rain or that a spirit is a bird; when, for example, a cucumber replaces the bull in a ritual, the cucumber is a bull, yet the bull is never a cucumber. In particular circumstances, defined by the religious tradition, signs *are* – instead of simply representing – what they signify.

To observe is to be related to something external which is to remain external . . . Piety is only for the pious, i.e., for him who *is* what he observes . . . To find the ground of religion (the philosophical thought) must abandon the relation of observing . . . If observation seeks to observe the Infinite in its true nature, it must itself be infinite, i.e., no longer observation of the matter at hand but rather that matter itself.

G. W. F. Hegel, tr. E. L. Fackenheim

This is, indeed, what makes the world of myths a 'wholly other' world whose description seems untranslatable into speech designed to grasp physical events; it has different norms of identification, different laws of causality, and different rules for interpreting the concatenation of phenomena. The 'participation' of people and things in this non-physical order may be, of course, easily dismissed as a pathology of speech (in accordance with Max Muller's old theory) or (this is how Cassirer would have it) as the mental relic of a hypothetical archaic era when men failed to distinguish between objects and symbols, i.e., when they were unaware of the semantic functions of speech. Such explanations are purely speculative contrivances. Muller's theory, as it stood, has been almost entirely forgotten, yet empiricist philosophers have revived it in a corrected version: religious beliefs may be interpreted as a pathology of speech in the sense that what keeps them alive is a failure to discriminate between meaningful and meaningless utter- ances according to the criteria of verifiability. This version, if it is supposed to be a genetic explanation, is not improved at all so far as its speculative character is concerned; if it is a norm stating the criteria of meaning, then the foregoing remarks on its arbitrariness need only be repeated. As to the theory implying that our ancestors were incapable of distinguishing a tree from the word 'tree' and that the persistence of religion may be accounted for by our continuing incapacity to make such distinctions in certain cases, there is no empirical evidence for it, and the theory is not credible as a common-sense truth.

The above-mentioned convergence of understanding and believing – both swallowed up in the act of 'participation' – may be observed in all religious rituals. As Mircea Eliade has repeatedly stressed, all of them, as long as they are taken seriously by believers, are taken as the genuine recreation of an original event, and not as acts of remembrance alone. The principal rite of Christianity, the Eucharist, may provide a good example, since it has so often served the rationalist critics as a favourite target for derision. Christians have never maintained that the words 'this is my flesh' suggest mysterious chemical processes whereby the bread is con- verted into flesh, and that one day we would observe the transmutation; they have always known that no empirical change of this kind occurs. On the other hand they have believed that the meaning of the ritual does not consist simply in recalling Christ's passion, but that through it they gain a real communion with the full life of the Redeemer, with His human and with His divine qualities. The later standard 'explanation' of the ritual in Aristotelian terms – the substance of bread is replaced by the substance of flesh while the accidents, i.e., the sense qualities, do not alter – did not pretend to have any empirical meaning either. The phrasing was perhaps unfortunate in terms of the continuity of religious tradition, as it was bound to fall victim to the general assault on the Aristotelian-scholastic conceptual network. But it soon became evident that all the endless attempts of sixteenth- and seventeenth-century controversialists to invent an amended formula would lead to greater and greater confusion. Luther said 'bread is flesh' which the Catholics said was nonsense – bread cannot be flesh and Jesus did not say *'panis est corpus meum'* but *'hoc est corpus meum'*. In Calvin's writings we can follow a number of more and more complicated formulae, apparently incompatible with each other and desperately aiming at a coherent and clear explanation – an unattainable goal. The radicals of the Reformation, starting with Zwingli, were increasingly ready to give up any attempt to clarify the way in which the 'real presence' of Christ in the Holy Communion is thinkable at all, and to reduce the ritual to a mere act of remembrance, thereby depriving it of its religious sense. It could not, by any ingenious linguistic manipulation, be given a form which might remotely meet profane standards of intelligibility. This is not to say, however, that what was supposed to happen in the ritual was intrinsically meaningless. It was understandable to believers within the framework of the entire system of ritual symbols; all acts of communication with a numinous reality belong within this system and none of them is in a better or worse position from the standpoint of norms governing profane perception or thinking.

To say that we have here to do with a metaphor does not help much, since we normally speak of a metaphorical expression when we know roughly how to reduce it to a non-metaphorical one, even if we admit that this reduction often involves impoverishment of one kind or another. In the case under scrutiny such a reduction is not feasible, and it would

When one sees Eternity in things that pass away and
Infinity in finite things, then one has pure knowledge. But
if one merely sees the diversity of things, with their
divisions and limitations, then one has impure knowledge. And if one selfishly sees a thing as if it were
everything, independent of the One and the many, then
one is in the darkness of ignorance.

From: The Bhagavad-Gita, *15*, *tr. J. Mascaró*

run against the original meaning of the ritual to attempt it.
Christians, while explaining the sense of the Eucharist or of
other rituals, have not spoken metaphorically; they have
had in mind real events which are not empirically testable
but conform to the ways God uses to contact human minds.
Those theologians and reformers who sought a compromise
with the requirements of empiricists and logicians and
devised 'improved' formulations, more palatable to the
taste of critics, entered a cul-de-sac. If they wanted to retain
the original sense of the ritual, simply rephrasing it in an
idiom better fitting the philosophical patterns of their time,
they could achieve nothing except to explain *ignotum per
ignotius*, and the history of the controversies on the
Eucharist in the period of the Reformation and Counter-
Reformation (and later) is one long list of such failures; and
if they were after a formula which the rationalist critics
would find flawless, the 'corrections' inevitably amounted to
suppressing totally the religious sense of religious speech.
The same may be said of all efforts to gain, for various
elements of sacred speech, the respectability of 'scientific'
discourse: in this respect the mystery of the Eucharist is in
the same position as the notion of grace, of the Holy Trinity
and, for that matter, of God.

On this occasion one can only repeat the question which
Erasmus and his followers were never tired of asking: why are

the Gospels so understandable to everybody except those whose minds have been corrupted by theological speculation? This is the case of all sacred texts of old, whether written or transmitted orally. The believers understand the language of the Sacred in its proper function, i.e., as an aspect of worship.

An objection can be raised at this point: 'a rational being cannot worship anything unless he first understands what it is.' This objection, however, arises from rationalist prejudices if it implies that one understands something to the extent that one is capable of giving an account of one's experience in terms which satisfy the norms of empiricism. Time and again we fall upon the same *petitio principii*: believers are told that their language is intrinsically unintelligible and that they themselves cannot understand it, and this because their language fails to meet the rules of intelligibility established by a philosophical ideology whose main purpose is to shape these rules in such a way as to exclude religious language from the realm of intelligibility. And, let us repeat, whatever the words 'rational' or 'irrational' signify hinges on the content we ascribe to the idea of *Ratio* and this, again, is entirely a matter of philosophical preference.

On the assumption that religious language is the speech of worship and that the knowledge of believers is guided, affirmed, kept alive and understood through acts of worship, one can easily come to the conclusion – quite common among less radical critics of religion – that this language is 'normative', 'expressive' or 'emotional'. A confusion readily emerges at this point, and the question whether or not and in what sense religious language is 'normative' is crucial in describing its peculiarity.

It has been mentioned that some mystics put an emphasis on the pragmatic, rather than the theoretical, meaning of our words when God and His attributes are spoken of; their intention was to point out the inadequacy of human tongues

> If hereby onely we know that we know Christ, by our keeping his Commandments, then the knowledge of Christ doth not consist merely in a few barren Notions, in a form of certain dry and saplesse Opinions . . . We say, Loe, here is Christ; and Loe, there is Christ, in these and these opinions; whereas in truth, Christ is neither here, nor there, nor any where; but where the Spirit of Christ, where the life of Christ is . . . Without purity and virtue God is nothing but an empty name; so it is as true here, that without obedience to Christ's Commandments, without the life of Christ dwelling in us, whatsoever opinions we entertain of him, Christ is but onely named by us, he is not known.
>
> *Ralph Cudworth (1647)*

in trying to cope with infinity, and by no means to find a profane sense for the sacred vocabulary; and, of course, not a shadow of doubt about God's reality was suggested, even if it turned out that the word 'nothing' suits Him as well as the word 'everything' (in the Buddhist tradition, including Zen, the theme of the divine Nothingness is perhaps more frequent). Whenever the 'normative' content of religious language is discussed in modern philosophy, it is not the mystical sense which is meant. The point is rather to say that religious utterances may be transposed into profane rules of behaviour whereby their *proper* sense is unveiled. Hobbes

> . . . God, if you talk about him without true virtue, is only a name.
>
> *Plotinus, tr. A. H. Armstrong*

was the most explicit: all the dogmas of Christian faith were to him merely the prescripts of political obedience and had no cognitive content whatever; the reason rulers employed this bizarre jargon to impose their sway over their subjects was again a matter of political expediency. When R. B. Braithwaite argues that Christian beliefs are indeed meaningful because they lead to important moral principles, he reverts to a very similar interpretation. The unverifiability of 'religious statements' does not deprive them of meaning, he thinks, if we decide to examine their content by looking at the actual use to which believers put them. And it turns out that they express a moral attitude or an intention to follow well defined rules of conduct; hence religious conviction is nothing but an act of allegiance to moral principles. This allegiance is supported by a specific 'story' of which the truth or falsity is, however, irrelevant to the authenticity of the belief.

This attempt to salvage the meaningfulness of religious beliefs by reducing them to moral precepts may be understood in two ways. Either it is an arbitrary decision, supported by standard empiricist definitions which make meaning dependent on verification procedures, or it is a psychological observation to the effect that religious people, when asserting their beliefs, do not have in mind anything else but their will to behave in a particular way. If the latter is the case, the observation is certainly false. When a Christian says that Jesus was God's son who descended upon earth to redeem the human race, it is obviously untrue to maintain that he in fact means *nothing more* than that he has decided to imitate Jesus's way of life. However his belief might be criticized by reference to the criteria of verifiability, it may not be reasonably stated, indeed it sounds absurd to state, that this belief *as he conceives of it* does not go beyond a moral programme. If, on the other hand, the suggested reduction is just a proposal for preserving from the religious legacy a portion of which an empiricist would be ready to say, 'I know what it means', then the proposal is simply a reiteration of the principles of empiricist doctrine. In all attempts to cut religious beliefs down to their normative consequences or to acts of moral will and moral commitment, everything specifically religious is left aside; this is not an interpretation but the outright dismissal of the language of the Sacred. To be sure, there is nothing logically inconsistent or psychologically impossible in saying, as many in fact do, 'I reject altogether all Christian beliefs concerning God, creation, salvation, etc., but I believe that the Christian moral rules are noble and I want to abide by them', yet such a decision is not a special interpretation – psychological, historical, or semantic – of Christianity; being a personal act of commitment, it does not help at all in understanding the meaning of religious speech.

The language of the Sacred is not normative in the semantic sense, as though it was 'ultimately' reducible to moral commandments with nothing more left. Nor is it normative in the psychological sense, i.e., in that people in fact receive religious myths as having *only* a 'prescriptive' content. And it would be obviously improper to label it normative and to mean that religious beliefs may be exhaustively described as a historical and cultural phenomenon in terms of their function in regulating human conduct. It would be improper, too, to say that in this language a logical connection occurs between mythical stories and theological statements on the one hand and moral norms on the other.

Still, there is a sense in which we may, if we wish, apply the label 'normative' to the language of the Sacred and this is an epistemological sense. I have to repeat a remark which concerns a question of primary importance in investigating the cognitive and the linguistic aspects of religious life. My claim is that there is a special kind of perception characteristic of the realm of the Sacred. In this realm the moral and the cognitive aspects of the act of perception are so blended that they are indistinguishable from each other: only an analysis 'from outside' produces this distinction. A believer

> The paradox of faith has lost the intermediate term, i.e.,
> the universal. On the one side it has the expression for the
> extremest egoism (doing the dreadful thing it does for
> one's own sake); on the other side it has the expression for
> the most absolute self-sacrifice (doing it for God's sake).
> Faith itself cannot be mediated into the universal, for it
> would thereby be destroyed. Faith is this paradox, and the
> individual absolutely cannot make himself intelligible to
> anybody.
>
> *Søren Kierkegaard, tr. W. Lowrie*

does not receive religious teaching in the form of mythical
tales or theoretical statements, out of which he subsequently proceeds to normative conclusions. The moral
content is given directly in the very act of perceiving and
understanding, for this act merges with moral commitment.
It is not the case that the believer separately 'knows' that
God is Creator and concludes that he ought to obey him
(such reasoning being logically illicit, anyway): he 'knows'
both in an act of acceptance. In religious acts of perceiving –
as opposed to theological speculation – there is hardly such a
thing as a pure 'factual statement': no particular verbal
expression is properly intelligible without being referred to
the entire space of a myth and none is meaningful in
religious terms without involving the acceptance of an
obligation. Let us repeat: religion is not a set of propositions,
it is the realm of worship wherein understanding, knowledge,
the feeling of participation in the ultimate reality (whether
or not a personal god is meant) and moral commitment
appear as a single act, whose subsequent segregation into
separate classes of metaphysical, moral and other assertions might be useful but is bound to distort the sense of the
original act of worship. In believing that Jesus offered
himself to save mankind from evil, a Christian does not

transubstantiate the accepted 'fact' into a normative conclusion to the effect that he ought to be grateful to the

---

It is only the knowledge of our duties and of the ultimate goal as the Reason defined it in them that could have produced in a determined way the concept of God; therefore this concept in its very origin is inseparable from our obligation towards this being.

Immanuel Kant

Redeemer and try to imitate, however imperfectly, His sacrifice in his own life: he perceives both directly. Isolated theological assertions like 'God exists' are not components of a religion, properly speaking; to admit God's existence as a theoretical proposition has little to do with genuinely religious acts of belonging; and Pascal was right in saying that deism was almost as remote from Christianity as atheism (many Christian writers who classified the varieties of atheism included on their list the attitude of people who admitted God's existence yet failed to display any signs proving that this knowledge is relevant to their life). A Hindu does not recognize the law of Karma in the same way he recognizes, say, the laws of thermodynamics: the latter can be learnt, understood, accepted for truth, logically connected with other known physical truths, employed in various technical manipulations; the former is understood as a religious truth in an act which involves, not only simultaneously but undistinguishably, the acceptance of one's own guilt, a feeling of belonging to a cosmic order and a commitment to conduct aiming at deliverance from the burden of the past and, eventually, from the wheel of changes. When God is spoken of as *Principium* and His word as Law, all the meanings of these words are intended: causal, moral and logical; and this is not a result of confusion or of logical carelessness. In the coalescence of all meanings the way of perception specific to the Sacred is reflected: cognitive insight, the feeling of being part of a universal order ruled by providential wisdom and the acceptance of a moral obligation are one.

This suggests that a religious myth (meaning not only the 'narrative' but the 'metaphysical' constituents of worship) can be understood only within, as it were, through real participation in a religious community. This was indeed Kierkegaard's claim: a non-Christian is unable to under-

---

There is a thing confusedly formed,
Born before heaven and earth.
Silent and void
It stands alone and does not change,
Goes around and does not weary.
It is capable of being the mother of the world.
I know not its name
So I style it 'the way'.

Lao Tzu, tr. D. C. Lau

---

stand Christianity. Such a rigorous formulation may be exaggerated; the process of so-called 'secularization' having flourished on a large scale for so relatively short a time, most non-believers in today's world were given a religious up-bringing and are still linked, though by a thin thread, to the religious tradition. Perhaps in discussing the question of understanding a strict either/or is improper, and we may admit that a half-understanding is conceivable (although many non-believers, including those educated in a pious milieu, peremptorily maintain that they do not understand religious language). Yet it is arguable that to people in whose minds all traces of traditional religious teaching have been erased and all forms of participation in rituals forgotten, the religious life proper, save for its 'secular' functions, does become unintelligible. If they try to make sense of it, they represent it as a collection of statements which, they inevitably conclude, are empty or illogical. The same can happen to religious people in encountering a civilization very remote from their own; thus in the eyes of many of the early missionaries and ethnographers who observed religious worship in primitive societies, the savages were simply stupid enough to imagine, say, that a man could be both a man and a parrot; these observers failed to notice that in terms of normal logical rules certain Christian tenets are hardly any better off.

Thus the language of myth is in a sense closed or self-supporting. People become participants in this communication system through initiation or conversion and not through a smooth transition and translation from the secular system of signs. Whatever people say in religious terms is understandable only by reference to the entire network of signs of the Sacred. Any example will serve to demonstrate this. Let us take a simple word from the religious vocabulary like 'sin'. Whoever says seriously 'I have sinned' does not mean merely that he has committed an act which is contrary to a law, but also that he has offended against God; his words are not meaningful unless they are referred to God and thus to the whole area of faith, hence they are bound to be considered unintelligible by a consistent non-believer. Besides, to the speaker his words, if uttered seriously, express repentance or at least disquietude. This is not to say that the sense of such a sentence is purely 'expressive', 'exclamatory' or 'prescriptive'; it does include a 'factual' statement, an assessment of the 'fact' in the full context of faith, and a personal emotional attitude. These three aspects of meaning can be singled out analytically, yet they are not separated in the speaker's mind, they are merged in one undifferentiated act of worship.

To admit that the language specifically designed to express the realm of the Sacred cannot be translated without distortion into the language of the Profane does not suggest at all that the latter, as opposed to the former, is natural, genuine, objective, descriptive, presuppositionless and apt to convey the truth. First, everyday profane speech teems with words which are value-laden or refer to unverifiable facts, in particular to our 'inner' states. A strictly 'empirical' or behaviourist language has never existed, it is an artificial concoction of philosophers and psychologists. Nor is it clear what purpose it might serve or of what benefit it might be. If we really wanted to follow the rules of such a language, we would be forbidden to say, e.g., 'he lied' (a reference to an unverifiable intention), 'he betrayed his friend' (a value judgement involved), 'I desire' (description of a 'subjective' state of affairs), etc. This is perhaps how B. F. Skinner would have it. The idea that such a construction is feasible or desirable implies that we can, in the language actually in use, make the distinction between a purely 'factual' or rigorously empirical content and other ('evaluative' or 'subjective') accretions, distil the former and throw away the latter as the cognitively empty debris of speech. In fact there are no reasons to maintain that in actual perception (as against the imaginary perception devised by behaviourists) the distinction between 'factual' and 'evaluative' content appears at all: when I see an evil action, I *see* an evil action and not movements which I subsequently interpret in a separate value judgement. When I observe a frightened man trying to escape from a burning house or an angry mother shouting at her capricious child, what I observe, oddly enough, is respectively a frightened man trying to escape from a burning house and an angry mother shouting at her capricious child, and not moving pictures which I fancy to be expressions of 'inner mental states' I put into others' bodies as a result of (logically inadmissible) projective reasoning, extrapolation, analogy, superstitious beliefs, etc. In other words, the moral qualities of human actions as well as their intentional background are not intellectual supplements to perception, they are perceived directly as aspects of a human sign system (my perception may be wrong, of course, as no perception is by its very content safeguarded against error).

Secondly, even if we succeeded in effectively designing and employing a behaviourist-empiricist language purged of all supposedly non-factual ingredients, we would still have no support for the claim that it is descriptive in the sense of being suitable to report what really happens without interferences from attitudes and 'normative' prejudices. An obstinate sceptic would still aver that the way this language selects qualities and events and the way it arranges the perceptual stuff is determined by the contingent biological endowment and historical vicissitudes of our species or that at any rate we are in principle incapable of separating this species-related contribution from the properties of the 'world in itself'. Both our perceptions and their verbal articulation would be, on this assumption, reduced to an instrumental or operational meaning and the question of 'objectivity' or 'truth' dismissed.

In short, we cannot prove that there is any non-historical, let alone transcendental, store of meaning preserved and reflected in historically shaped natural languages. If it exists, it cannot be discovered except by means the use of which has to presuppose its existence, according to the traditional sceptical argument. This is not to deny, though, or to minimize the difference between the ideal language of behaviourists or the actual language of secular life on the one side and the language of the Sacred on the other. Yet the difference is not in their 'objectivity' or in the access to truth they respectively provide or fail to provide. They serve different purposes: the former, in its purely 'empirical' aspects, is appropriate for reacting to and for manipulating our natural environment, the latter for making it intelligible; as a whole, the language of the Profane, including its re-sources for depicting the human world in terms of its moral and 'intentional' characteristics, enables communication in the realm of specifically human relationships. There is also a cognitive difference consisting in the degree of universality. So far as we can determine, the components of language with a clear empirical reference are universal in the sense that they are transferable from one civilization to another; perhaps the same may be said of elements involving the intentional interpretation of human behaviour. Expressions which imply a moral assessment of events are, for the most part, certainly less universal and independent of cultural norms; however we need not be concerned, just now, with the never-ending anthropological and philosophical debate on this subject. The language of the Sacred is not universal. This is to say that acts of worship do not retain their sacral sense in different civilizations; the words can be translated from one ethnic tongue into another, of course, yet not so their religious significance.

The arguments of those who try to uncover identical patterns in religious symbols across the whole variety of civilizations and systems of worship do not abolish the mutually exclusive nature of religions. Whatever truth they may contain, these arguments are the analytical performance of psychologists, anthropologists, and students of comparative religion; they are not religious acts in themselves. On the assumption that all the religions of the world are, as the Romantics held, historical and relative embodiments of some primordial revelation, a philosopher might well believe that various tribes, without knowing it, worship the same God through different rites. However, people do not worship abstract concepts or hidden archetypes. They cannot extract from their religions a universal hard-core, common to all human races and cultures, and disregard all the historical forms whereby they express it. If there is such an essence, for instance in mystical experience, it is inexpressible either in words or in a ritual. Jung's archetypes cannot be perceived as such, in their unadulterated purity, but only in historically and culturally specific manifestations. It is as impossible to perform acts of worship reduced to some hypothetical religious hard-core, universal and non-historical, as it is to paint a cat that would be the pure embodiment of felinity and thus have none of the characteristics which distinguish one cat from another. Actual worship is necessarily culture-bound. This would hold true even if, as the result of a conceivable though extremely unlikely process, mankind one day achieved religious unity: such an imaginary religion would be universal in the sense of being shared and understood all over the world, yet it would not cease to be historically and culturally relative; its symbols, rites and beliefs would not be distilled to some immutable elixir of Religiosity, but would abide within their cultural environment.

People are initiated into the understanding of a religious language and into worship through participation in the life of a religious community, rather than through rational persuasion. Alexander Safran, the chief rabbi of the city of Geneva, provides in his book *Die Kabbala* the following exposition of Judaic faith. The authenticity of God's word is preserved among Jews when it is being transmitted orally, rather than in writing; it has to be conveyed through a direct contact between master and disciple. The Jews believe, he says, that the understanding of Torah is possible only through partaking in the life of the Jewish people; the spoken text has priority over the script and the proper seat of the Torah is the memory of the faithful; the prophets themselves committed their message to the written word only under duress, when they were forbidden to speak publicly. This self-interpretation of Judaism bears out what might seem a common-sense truth: meaning is formed by acts of communication, and has to be recreated in those acts time and again and again.

Being different, yet not isolated, from profane communication, the language of worship cannot escape the impact of all the other aspects of the civilization within which it lives and changes, develops and withers away. What happens in politics, philosophy, science, customs, art, fashions, affects the way believers perceive their faith and express their communion with the mysterious *Numinosum*. Yet no religious life is conceivable without an underlying conviction that through all the mutations an unvarying and fundamental structure of worship persists. It makes itself felt in the content of beliefs, in the meaning of rituals, in the relationship between the Eternal and the Transient, in the very continuity of the religious body (in Christian terms: the permanent *corpus mysticum* contrasted with the changing historical forms of expression). These attempts to grasp the Immutable in the flow of changes naturally extend into language itself. Hence the yearning after a lost linguistic paradise, the temptation to rediscover, behind the variety of accidental vernaculars, language *par excellence*, the original tongue that preceded Babel. We find in many civiliza-

---

Of course, God need not protect Himself, but He does protect His name, and so seriously that He adds to this single commandment a special threat. This is done because, within the name, that which bears the name is present.

Paul Tillich

---

tions evidence of a nostalgic belief in an intrinsic, essential kinship between word and meaning and of an unending quest for the 'true' meaning and the 'true' language spoken at the beginning of time. Linguistically this is nonsense, to be sure: the meaning of words is determined by convention and historical accidents and, apart from actual usage, there is no 'genuine' tongue, no veritable meaning and no mysterious affinity between things and names. Yet the myth of Babel is deeply rooted in our linguistic consciousness; we want to recover the lost, original, God-given speech in which things are called by *their* names, their celestial proper names. This belief and this quest manifest themselves and can be traced in magic, in rituals, in Cabbalistic explorations, in the entire esoteric tradition, in the very concept of a holy language. Nor is contemporary philosophy free from the temptation. When Heidegger says '*die Sprache spricht*' (the speech speaks) or '*Die Sprache ist das Haus des Seins*' (the speech is the house of Being), what he apparently means is both that one can arrive at a knowledge of the genuine meaning of words and so penetrate into the essence of things (which he repeatedly tried to do in analysing the Greek and German roots of the philosophical vocabulary), and that things are born together with their names; this is hinted at in the poem by Stefan George he quotes: '*kein ding sei, wo das wort gebricht*' (let no thing be where the word is missing).

And so, in the religious approach to language we detect the same inspiration that pervades all forms of worship: a desire to escape the misery of contingency, to force the door to a kingdom which resists the voracity of time.

I have been trying to point out a few aspects of the differences between *sacrum* and *profanum* in the realm of language. To say that in the sacred language, as against the profane, the act of understanding merges with the act of believing, and believing with moral commitment is to suggest that in the religious realm the fact/value distinction either looks different from the way it looks in secular life or does not appear at all. This is indeed the case. The fact/value dichotomy is a cultural fact. People realized, as a result of encounters with other customs and civilizations, that some areas of perception and some forms of thinking are shared universally, or at least universally enough to relegate the few individuals who refuse to share them to the social limbo of madness; meanwhile other areas, in particular myths, and judgements about what is morally right or wrong, do not enjoy this kind of universality. This field of irreducible disagreement was, in antiquity, already given a separate epistemological status, and later on, with the development of empiricist philosophy, the question of its validity was to be dismissed as a non-question. The unspoken reason for this dismissal was precisely the historical fact of actual irreconcilable divergence of opinion among various cultural traditions. But for this fact we would not have noticed that the realm of moral norms and values had an epistemological position of its own; indeed we would have had no reason to notice it: the distinction would simply not have emerged. The area of quasi-universal agreement was identified as a domain wherein truth and falsity may be reasonably spoken of, and this for no better reason than the very fact of agreement. Later on there was a conceptual leap from this fact of universal agreement to validity in a transcendental sense, and the awareness of this shift has been conspicuously absent in the less radical empiricist tradition (the radical current admitted it and thus it was ready to jettison the idea of truth altogether and to be satisfied with pragmatic rules of admissibility). Thus the separation of values from 'descriptive' assertions was a cultural fact which later acquired an epistemological significance. Yet, once the distinction appeared it could not be cancelled.

What is *Morally* filthy, should be Equivalent to what is *Naturally* Impossible: we *should not*, is morally we *can not*.

Benjamin Whichcote

It could not be cancelled in the profane tongue, that is. It did not emerge in the language of the sacred. Once we have access to the ultimate source of truth there is no need for it and no place where it might appear. In the realm of sacred speech, whether an assertion has an ostensibly 'descriptive' or 'normative' form, it has the same validity and this for two

reasons. First, because the criteria of validity are the same.
It is God's explicit word, or primordial revelation, or the
wisdom gained in a special kind of enlightenment. Whatever
comes from this source is equally valid, whether it says, for
instance, that there is only one God or that one ought to
obey Him. Secondly, because, in accordance with the above-
mentioned pattern of the perception of the Sacred, the two
kinds of knowledge merge in one. Within this perception the
statement that it is wrong to kill is true in exactly the same
sense as the statement that wrongdoers, as a matter of fact,
will be punished by God. This is not to say that we have to do
with two logically equivalent assertions: rather with two
sides of one perceptual act.

Therefore the standard argument which is advanced on
such occasions by analytical philosophers – 'the statement
that God exists, true or false, is descriptive, consequently no
normative judgements may be validly inferred from it' – is
pointless in the religious perspective. It implies premises
which are arbitrary and inapplicable: religious perception
does not generate special prescriptions of logical alchemy
whereby certain matter-of-fact statements might be trans-
muted into moral norms. The very distinction is absent. It
does exist, and it ought not to be obscured, in the language of
science.

Not only is it proper to say that in terms of religious
perception judgements about what is morally right or wrong
are true or false; it can be argued that the inverse holds good
also. This means that judgements about what is right or
wrong, good or evil, may be validated only in terms of the
sacred language, which amounts to repeating the saying 'if
there is no God everything is permissible'. The possible
epistemological significance of this saying has been discussed already but its moral meaning – which, of course, it
originally intended – seems to be equally defensible.

I have been arguing that in everyday speech a clear separation of purely 'empirical' expressions from value-loaded

ones fails to appear, that many events which involve human actions display their moral qualities directly to our perception and that we describe them in words which carry an ineluctable moral assessment. This might suggest that we do not need any sacred authority, an infallible other-worldly judge in order to gain certainty about our moral opinions since they are, as it were, not opinions at all but aspects of our perceptual acts.

This is not so, alas. What I think about how good and evil can be recognized and distinguished from each other is not only in fact denied by some other people but may be challenged as a matter of principle, and this challenge is unanswerable if it really is levelled at the very criteria of good and evil and not at the ways in which they are or can be achieved. If it is true that my criteria do not need to be explicit and are somehow built into my acts of perception and into my manner of describing human affairs in everyday speech, they may be dismissed all the same; and often I *am* powerless to reply to this challenge by appealing to some common ground I share with my adversary. I may perceive, say, the evil of killing malformed babies, but I have to admit that this kind of perception is not universal and that people in other civilizations – which I am perfectly entitled to describe in pejorative terms and call barbarous – see things differently. Thus if it is true that a strictly empirical or behaviourist language is a *figmentum rationis* and cannot operate in everyday life, it is also true that the morally loaded ingredients of our speech do not need to be and are not in fact identical through human history and geography. I may presume – although this presumption does not seem to be provable or disprovable – that the way people perceive and describe facts in moral terms is an aspect of their participation in the realm of the sacred and that among non-believers this kind of perception is the residue of a particular religious legacy they inescapably share by the very fact of having been brought up in a particular civilization. This is a matter for anthropological and historical inquiry (probably unfeasible) and I shall set it aside.

The question of validity, though, is logically independent of it. For centuries the forging of a scientific language has been accompanied by an increasingly consistent effort to cleanse it from all value- and goal-oriented as well as from 'subjective' and intention-related components. This work of purification has been progressing inexorably, spreading from physics to chemistry and biology, and its most recent phase (in rough conformity with the Comtean hierarchy of science) has been the emergence of behaviourist psychology and sociology. Its encroachment upon historical studies has been quite modest and most likely will never be entirely successful or the latter ceased to be what they are meant to be: the description of unique and unrepeatable chains of human actions, including people's goals, passions, desires and fears (the recent impressive advances in quantitive historiography have brought no changes in this respect). I have argued that the language of science may not make claims to provide access to truth considered in a transcendental sense (unless arbitrary philosophical presuppositions are implicitly admitted or, again, the very legitimacy of the concept of truth is supported by the appeal to an omniscient being). Even so, its advantages and its superiority consist in its appeal to the patterns of thinking (i.e., logical rules) and of perception which, we may reasonably believe, are universal and in this sense may be called 'objective'. The claim can be made that this language prescribes the criteria of admissibility which people are likely to come to an agreement upon. A language which involves historically shaped value judgements is not supported by such a higher tribunal capable of an 'intersubjective' assessment of controversies, and therefore its presuppositions may be contested not only by paranoiacs but by people who belong to a different cultural tradition (the epistemological status of the paranoiac is ultimately reducible to the fact that he is alone).

And this is the sense in which the saying 'if there is no God, everything is permissible' seems right to me. We have to accept the empiricists' contention (in a phrasing which is somewhat restricted yet sufficient for this purpose) that our judgements about what is morally good or evil cannot have logical equivalents in assertions formulated in a language which lacks such predicates, especially in the language of empirical science. The solution suggested by some philosophers – 'we can know what is good or evil by examining the way people use those adjectives' – will not do, considering that people do not use them in the same way always and everywhere. For the same reason we cannot seek refuge in a supposed universally human intuition with which we might lodge our appeal when a clash arises between conflicting moral views.

Can we expect to lay the foundations of a rational normative code without appealing either to an innate moral insight or to a divine authority, granted that the former seems to be disproved and the latter unprovable? It is not plausible. Kant's theory of practical reason has remained perhaps the boldest attempt to find an independent and unquestionable source of moral certainty and, even though this certainty was limited to the formal conditions on which material moral commandments might be admissible at all, and could not confer validity directly on those commandments themselves, the idea appears unsound. The validity of the famous formal Kantian demand – I ought to act only according to a principle which I could wish to be a general law – was grounded on the fact that I cannot be consistent in acting otherwise, and that a principle of conduct which does not observe this restriction is self-defeating. If, for instance, my conduct is guided by a principle which allows me to lie whenever it suits me, then my principle justifies anybody else's lying and yet, when everybody is entitled to lie, nobody is believed any more and no liar achieves his goal; consequently the principle undermines itself.

This reasoning is not convincing and perhaps circular. Even on the assumption that some principles – no matter whether or not explicitly admitted – necessarily underlie my conduct, i.e., that whatever I do I am bound to believe, however vaguely, in a normative 'principle' which justifies my acts (and the assumption is far from obvious), there is no reason why those principles should necessarily be of universal validity and why I must, so to speak, impose my own rules on the whole of mankind (not only Kant shared this opinion; so did Sartre, for reasons not explained). I am not inconsistent at all if I prefer other people to follow rules which I do not want to abide by. If – to continue the example given above – I lie whenever it pleases me but I wish everyone else to remain invariably truthful, I am perfectly consistent. I may always, without contradicting myself, dismiss the arguments of people who try to convert me or prompt me to mend my ways by asking me 'what if everybody did the same?', because I can consistently reply either that I do not care about others' conduct or that I positively wish them to obey norms which I refuse to observe.

In other words, an imperative demanding that I be guided only by norms which I might wish to be universal has itself no logical or psychological foundation; I can reject it without falling into contradiction, and I may admit it as a supreme guideline only by virtue of an arbitrary decision unless it appears within the context of religious worship.

A proviso may be useful at this point. To say that moral criteria cannot be ultimately validated without an appeal to the repository of transcendent wisdom is not to suggest any theory about anthropological or psychological connections between morals and religious beliefs. The two sets of questions are logically independent. In refuting attempts to produce a morality independent of religious worship I have in mind the question of validity only. There is in this argument no ground for stating that in moral affairs non-believers cannot, as a matter of fact, perform as well as or better than believers; nor does the argument imply any theory about how moral ideas and conduct were historically dependent on myths. Least of all does it suggest that religious beliefs, under various historical circumstances, cannot be employed to justify actions which, by almost any standards, appear morally repugnant. Anthropological, historical and psychological questions of this kind do not properly belong here and are only cursorily mentioned. The point is simply to note that the celebrated idea of an 'independent ethics' may include a number of issues which are logically separable from each other and are to be dealt with severally. When Pierre Bayle argued that morality does not depend on religion, he was speaking mainly of psychological independence; he pointed out that atheists are capable of achieving the highest moral standards (Spinoza was to him an eminent example; occasionally Vanini) and of putting to shame most of the faithful Christians. That is obviously true as far as it goes, but this matter-of-fact argument leaves the question of validity intact; neither does it solve the question of the effective sources of the moral strength and moral convictions of those 'virtuous pagans'. A Christian apologist may admit the facts and still consistently argue not only that atheists owe their virtues to a religious tradition they have managed partially to preserve in spite of their false philosophy but that those virtues, even in their case, were God's gifts (this might sound incredible, especially in the case of Vanini, whose virtues were clearly at the service of godlessness and could only perplex simple believers; but in an apologist's eyes God's inscrutable ways can always be plausibly defended: He often confuses people in order to try their faith and a virtuous or seemingly virtuous envoy of hell might be as well employed for His plans as a villainous pope).

And yet the really burning question in the area of relationships between religious and moral life is not that of epistemological validity. In discussing moral issues people (as distinct from philosophers) do not really worry much about the ultimate provability of normative propositions; neither is it likely that if they were taught that validation procedures can indeed be properly carried out, this would change their patterns of moral behaviour. I might be convinced that statements about good and evil are true or false (which I indeed believe to be the case) and still ignore the truth with impunity, at least in empirical chains of events, which I could not afford to do if empirical or mathematical truths were at stake. By ignoring or refusing to admit a truth of the kind 'the consumption of alcohol is damaging to the liver' or 'two and two are four' I incur a well-defined risk, which shows me that I am not able to cancel such truths by arbitrary decree. Yet I can freely abrogate the truth of the kind 'envy is wrong' and not be punished by any natural causality.

Moral beliefs, not being testable or refutable in the same way as empirical beliefs, are also differently acquired. The qualities of good and evil are arguably perceived directly in everyday experience, yet this does not entail that the ability to recognize them is formed in our minds through a process similar to learning to discriminate between red and yellow. Even if purely intellectual persuasion could induce me to admit that the statement 'envy is wrong' is indeed true, I would still be perfectly capable of ignoring this truth in my behaviour and of claiming that in doing so I am not inconsistent. We do not assent to our moral beliefs by admitting 'this is true' but by feeling guilty if we fail to comply with them.

According both to the Bible and to Sigmund Freud the capacity for guilt has constituted the human race as we know it. The ability to experience guilt does not follow upon the assertion of the rightness of such or another value judgement, nor of course can it be identified with the fear of legal punishment. It is not an intellectual performance but an act of questioning one's own status in the cosmic order (an 'existential' act, I would say, if I did not dislike the adjective); it is not a fear of revenge but a feeling of awe in the face of one's own action which has disturbed the world-harmony, an anxiety following the transgression *not of a law* but of a *taboo*. It is not only I who am threatened by the enormity of my defiance: the universe as a whole is threatened, plunged as it were into chaos and uncertainty.

The presence of taboo is both the immovable pillar of *any* viable moral system (as distinct from a penal one) and an integral component of religious life; thus taboo is a necessary link binding the worship of eternal reality with the

---

The concept of guilt and punishment, the entire 'moral world-order', was invented *in opposition to* science – *in opposition to* the detaching of man from the priest . . . Man shall *not* look around him, he shall look down into himself; he shall not look prudently and cautiously into things in order to learn, he shall not look at all: he shall *suffer* . . . And he shall suffer in such a way that he has need of the priest at all times. – Away with physicians! *One has need of a Saviour.* – The concept of guilt and punishment, including the doctrine of 'grace', of 'redemption', of 'forgiveness' – *lies* through and through and without any psychological reality – were invented to destroy the *causal sense* of man: they are outrage on the concept of cause and effect!

Friedrich Nietzsche, tr. R. J. Hollingdale

---

knowledge of good and evil. This worship and this knowledge operate conjointly and neither is viable without the other. Religion is neither a collection of statements about God, Providence, heaven and hell, nor is morality a codified set of normative utterances, but a lived allegiance to an order of taboos. This is the reason why one is so often overwhelmed with a feeling of sterility in perusing the countless number of books and articles by modern philosophers looking for some recipe whereby 'descriptive judgements' might be magically converted into 'normative' ones and the truth or falsity of the latter demonstrated. The same sterility haunts the opposite camp of philosophers who argue that such a feat is impracticable. All such endeavours are pathetically irrelevant to what moral life is about; on the unlikely assumption that they succeed and that philosophers will indeed convincingly perform the desired conversion, there is still no ground to expect that anything would change in human behaviour. Let us suppose that I am an inveterate and uninhibited liar and that a benevolent and philanthropic philosopher succeeds in convincing me that the statement 'lying is wrong' is true in the same sense as Heisenberg's principle; what reasons would I have to quit my deplorable habit provided that I can indulge in it with impunity, and what might prevent me from shrugging off this new scientific discovery by saying that I do not care? As long as moral motivations

---

Good works do not make a good man, but a good man does good works; evil works do not make a wicked man, but a wicked man does evil works. Consequently it is always necessary that the substance or person himself be good before there can be any good works, and that good works follow and proceed from the good person . . .

Martin Luther, tr. W. A. Lambert

---

work at all in our patterns of conduct, they work not because the corresponding value judgements have been reliably inferred, to our satisfaction, from empirical propositions, but because we are capable of feeling guilty. The consciousness of guilt is the counterpart of taboo, whereas the fear of punishment is related to the force of law; the two kinds of motivation and two kinds of inhibition must not be confused; they differ in psychological, as well as in anthropological, terms. This is why there are no grounds to expect that in a society where all taboos have been done away with, and consequently the consciousness of guilt has evaporated (and both can obviously continue to operate for a time, by the inertial force of tradition, after religious beliefs have vanished from people's minds), only legal coercion would remain to keep the entire fabric of communal life from falling apart and all non-coercive human bonds from dissolving. Such a society has never existed in a perfect form and it took the genius of Hobbes to anticipate it in his 'geometrical' model; this model, albeit viewed by Hobbes himself as a reconstruction of reality, may be defined precisely in the terms just suggested: as a society without taboos.

Even though we have made impressive progress, since the seventeenth century, towards this kind of society, we still do not know for sure whether it would be viable or not and what it would look like; we have no instruments to measure the living force – or the vestigial inertia – of the old taboos and of corresponding inhibitions in keeping human communities together; yet we have good reasons to guess that their role in social relationships is quite substantial.

And the taboo resides in the kingdom of the Sacred. Whatever its actual content in a given society and whatever its 'ultimate' origin, it is – and I am merely repeating a very traditional tenet – irreducible to, and inexpressible in terms of, all other forms of human communication; it is *sui generis* both in the perception of those who feel its presence and in reality. No matter how frequently violated, taboos are alive as long as their violation produces the phenomenon of guilt. Guilt is all mankind has, save for sheer physical compulsion, to impose rules of conduct on its members, and all it has to give those rules the form of moral commandments. Even on the unprovable premise that taboos do in fact 'express' biological inhibitions (unprovable because of the enormous variety of the former) the very fact that these inhibitions have had to take the shape of sacred orders would suggest that they have largely lost their persuasive power as instinctual behaviour patterns. In a word, culture *is* taboos or, to put it another way, a culture without taboos is a square circle. In accepting that, we do not need to give credence either to Freud's self-contradictory story about the origin of taboos or to those variants of naturalistic philosophy which conceive of culture as a substitute for instincts.

But the essence of repression lies in a necessary turning away from direct and conscious expression of everything that is before praise and blame. A culture without repression, if it could exist, would kill itself in closing the distance between any desire and its object. Everything thought or felt would be done, on the instant. Culture is the achievement of its unconscious distancing devices made conscious, yet indirect, in a variety of visual, acoustical, and plastic registrations. In a word, culture is repressive.

Philip Rieff

I am not trying to venture into the precincts of anthropologists. I want to stress, though, that the link tying our perception of good and evil to the realm of the Sacred is stronger than any semantic discussion might suggest, and that this link is displayed in the very concept of culture (and the way this concept is to be built is not a matter for anthropological, empirical inquiry; it does involve philosophical options). It might be true, as anthropologists argue, that theological ideas are not necessarily the carriers of moral beliefs, since in various archaic religions the gods are not at all depicted as models of conduct to be imitated by humans. Yet it is the very existence of taboos that matters and not whether the gods are themselves bound to obey them.

The great monotheistic religions, especially after their philosophical elaboration in the neo-platonic conceptual *instrumentarium* (Christianity and Islam underwent this treatment, and Judaism too, to a certain extent), revealed a curious asymmetry in the way they established the distinction between good and evil. On the one hand the idea of the single good Creator naturally implies that whatever is, is good; thus evil has no positive reality and is to be seen as a pure lack, *carentia*, an ontological hole, so to speak. Evil is the absence of something that ought to be, therefore we can know and define evil only by reference to God or Being. Logically the good has a compelling precedence; evil or non-being is conceptually dependent on good. In this sense they are asymmetrical.

Although, therefore, evil, in so far as it is evil, is not a good; yet the fact that evil as well as good exists, is a good. For if it were not a good that evil should exist, its existence would not be permitted by the omnipotent God.

St Augustine, tr. J. F. Show

The opposite is the case, however, in the way that the tree of knowledge enters our experience. In an experience which is not enlightened by divine wisdom, good and evil, as distinct from pleasure and pain, do not appear: we may know suffering, fear and death but we know them as natural facts, as something to be avoided. We owe the moral distinction to our participation in taboos. And the distinction appears in experience as a result of those of our acts which violate a taboo and thus bring disorder into the world. In other words, we really know what is good by knowing what is evil and we know evil by doing it. In experience, evil has to come first as against the sequence represented in theological speculation. And the first evil I can know is the evil in me, whereas evil in others (again: as distinct from natural facts) is derivative.

In the experience of failure, in seeing Being defeated by nothing, the knowledge of Being and of good emerges. By becoming evil myself I know what evil is and then what good is. Once again conceptualization and experience move in opposite directions on the path of knowledge: the mystics were aware of that. The God of Genesis saw that His creation was good, yet the creatures lacked this knowledge. Our primogenitors had to do evil before they knew what good and evil was; their sin led them to knowledge and made them human.

This may be expressed in a more general way: the Sacred is revealed to us in the experience of our failure. Religion is indeed the awareness of human insufficiency, it is lived in the admission of weakness. This was what made Christianity so hateful to Nietzsche, as his *Anti-Christ* and other writings testify. In his eyes Christianity (and the Judaism of which it was the ultimate offspring) was a sickness, an expression of envy and resentment by those who, being poorly endowed with life force and unable to survive in the struggle, had to invent an ideology glorifying weakness, meekness and intellectual poverty; this inept race was a foe of Nature and its vested interest was to suppress and to denigrate the noble prowess of instinct and to assert their own debility as a mark of the Elected. They contrived the idea of guilt, of remorse, of redemption, of grace and forgiveness, they extolled the virtues of humility and self-debasement, in order to pull mankind down to their own wretched level, to infect the higher race with their instinct-hating values and thereby to assure the triumph of their Chandala-like infirmity over the healthy vigour of life.

Christianity was to Nietzsche a rebellion of the withered branch against the resilient tree. One may only wonder how this envious frailty could prove to be victorious against the élan of robust 'life'. It would rather seem that the weak, if they succeed in imposing their values on the world – however circuitous and cunning their tactics – prove not to be weak after all, in accordance with Nietzsche's own criteria: there is no 'rightness' other than strength and vitality. Since he glorifies the innocence of the natural process – *Unschuld des Werdens* – and affirms the perfection of the world as it is, scornfully rejecting the idea of what it ought to be, it might seem that the winners are right by definition – and the Christians were winners. This is only one among his numerous inconsistencies. He glorified the infallibility of instinct and, in the same breath, the greatness of science and of scepticism; thus he suggested that scepticism might be the result of instinct or that instinct naturally produced sceptical attitudes!

Still, it would be too easy to dismiss Nietzsche's anti-Christian fury as a mere presage of his oncoming madness. Absurd as it might have been to denounce envy and resentment as the roots of Christianity – the entire text of the Gospels is an irrefutable argument against this indictment – it was not at all absurd to see in it a confession of irreparable human infirmity. It does not take, however, a clever philosopher to unmask this side of Christianity, for this is what it says about itself. Sickness is the natural state of a Christian, Pascal wrote to his sister, Madame Perrier. Christianity may be viewed as an expression of what in human misery is incurable by human efforts; an expression, rather than a philosophical or psychological description. Thereby it *is* a cry for help. By making people acutely aware of their contingency and the finitude of life, of the corruptibility of the body, of the limitations of reason and language, of the power of evil in us, and by concentrating this awareness in the doctrine of original sin, Christianity clearly defied the Promethean side of the Enlightenment and was to be inevitably castigated for its 'anti-humanist' bias. To what extent this accusation is justified – and indeed in what sense it amounts to an accusation – depends on the meaning of the word 'humanism', and all the known definitions of it are heavily loaded with ideological content. If 'humanism' means a doctrine implying either that there are no limits whatever to human self-perfectibility or that people are entirely free in stating the criteria of good and evil, Christianity is certainly opposed to humanism. It does not follow that it is anti-human, unless we believe that the ideology of humanism in the sense just defined favours as a matter of fact those values which make people better and happier. If those values are the same we appeal to in defining humanism, then this assumption is tautologically true and therefore empty. If not, the question may be empirical. And empirically it is far from obvious that humanism in its radically anti-Christian version – i.e., that which implies that the human race does not find any criteria of good and evil ready-made but may fashion them as it pleases – produces a better, less aggressive and less suffering human community. Recent history seems rather to suggest that attempts, in traditionally Christian societies, to achieve a perfect 'liberation' from what radical humanists believed was man's bondage under God's imaginary tyranny, were to threaten mankind with a more sinister slavery than Christianity had ever encouraged.

However, historical speculation is not topical to this discussion. The point is only to repeat that Christianity is indeed the expression of what is lasting in human misery and weakness. It does imply that in moral matters our choices are limited in the sense that the basic rules distinguishing good from evil do not originate in the free decision of men but have been given us by an authority which we may not dispute; and it teaches that there are sources of suffering which are, as it were, ontological and thus unremovable, that more often than not we heal our misfortunes with medicaments that produce more disease, and that the ultimate cure or salvation is beyond our reach and can only be secured by the divine healer.

Yet in this general sense any religion, religion as such, is 'anti-humanist' or anti-Promethean. The very phenomenon of the Sacred and the very act of worship express man's awareness of his lack of self-sufficiency, of both an ontological and a moral weakness which he is not strong enough to overcome alone. The religious literature of all civilizations amply testifies to this and supremely so in such immortal monuments of spirit as the book of Job and the Gospels. And this is what the great prophets of atheism – from Lucretius to Feuerbach and Nietzsche – were keenly aware of; they did not deny the fact of human infirmity, yet they refused, at least many of them, to admit its ontological permanence. The invariable message of Promethean atheism is: 'human self-creativity has no limits, evil and suffering are contingent, life is infinitely inventive, nothing is valid – morally or intellectually – just because it has passed for valid throughout history, there is no authority in tradition, the human mind does not need any revelation or any teaching from without, God is but man oppressing himself and stifling his reason.' The invariable message of religious worship is 'from the finite to the infinite the distance is always infinite; whatever we create is doomed to perish sooner or later, life is doomed to failure, and death is insuperable unless we have a part in the eternal reality which is not of our producing but on which we depend; we can perceive it, however dimly and inadequately, and it is the source of all our knowledge of good and evil; otherwise we are left alone with our passions to acquire the rules of good and evil, and more often than not, our passions are evil and make us foes to one another; nothing can curb them except trust in the veracity of God's revelation of Himself.'

And so, we face two irreconcilable ways of accepting the world and our position in it, neither of which may boast of being more 'rational' than the other; in confronting them we face an option; once taken, any choice imposes criteria of judgement which infallibly support it in a circular logic: if there is no God, empirical criteria alone have to guide our thinking, and empirical criteria do not lead to God; if God

exists, He gives us clues about how to perceive His hand in
the course of events, and with the help of those clues we
recognize the divine sense of whatever happens. An analogous circularity is involved in moral matters: if God gives us
standards of good and evil, we can prove that those who
reject God do evil; if there is no God, we freely decide how
those standards have to be set up and whatever we do, we can
always prove to be good.

The atheists may argue that if mankind had not rebelled
against the tyranny of myths, if it had passively submitted to
the rigid principles they imposed, it would never have been
able to unfold its intellectual and cultural potentialities. The
defenders of the religious legacy may argue that, on the
contrary, arts, literature and even technical skills had been
developing for centuries largely within a religious context
(are not the most lasting achievements of architecture the
monuments of faith: temples and tombs? Are not the sacred
texts of old the most exquisite products of mind? etc.) and
that conservative confidence in the religious tradition is the
only reliable way of keeping alive the distinction between
good and evil.

The two options just sketched are mutually exclusive but
not exhaustive. It is possible to say that there is neither
Providence to help us nor infinite human self-creativity to
lead us towards perfection and that we have to face defeat as
the ultimate outcome of all human efforts. This noblest and
most lucid form of atheism, thought by Lucretius, by Marcus
Aurelius, by Schopenhauer, by Jaspers, leaves the question
open: may the concept of metaphysical defeat be validated
at all in the atheist perspective? May the spurious escape
from despair – the *amor fati* of Stoics?

Let us repeat: such dilemmas have little to do with the
legitimacy of belief or unbelief in terms of scientific canons.
From all the irrefutable testimonies of human misery there
is no logically sound path to the great heavenly Physician;
from the fact that we are sick it does not follow that we can be

cured. It is possible, as Pascal repeatedly argued, that the human condition, including all its sorrows and evils, as well as its splendours and greatness, is unintelligible and meaningless unless it is seen in the light of sacred history: creation, sin, redemption. If so, it appears that the admissible options are: a meaningful world guided by God, spoilt by men, healed by the Redeemer; or an absurd world, going Nowhere, ending in Nothing, the futile toy of an impersonal Fate which does not distribute punishments and rewards and does not care about good and evil. Promethean atheism might appear, on this assumption, a puerile delusion, an image of a godless world which rushes on to the Ultimate Hilarity. This solution being set aside, we are left with the two options just mentioned but with no further intellectually reliable guidance in making a choice between them. God gives the world meaning, makes it intelligible, but He does not explain it in the normal sense of the word (as an earthquake is explained by tectonic shifts). And *prima facie* there is nothing absurd in believing that the world *is* absurd.

Pascal went further. He argued that opting for God is reasonable on practical grounds. In the famous *pari* he tried to use the reasoning a gambler applies at the roulette table. The analogy breaks down at one important point, though: a gambler can simply leave the game whereas everyone has to bet for God or against Him, nobody can withdraw from the terrible *divertissement*, there is no way to avoid the choice between a life based on the belief in God and conduct implying His absence. Once the coercion of gambling is established, one has to draw the balance of risks and gains. The risk is certain, the loss and the gain uncertain, as in any game of chance. In betting on God – on the assumption that His existence is uncertain – we might gain an infinite life of happiness; meanwhile at stake is our finite life with its futile pleasures. A finite stake against the chance of infinite gain or a finite gain against the chance of an eternity of agony: what creature endowed with reason could hesitate?

This exhortation is subject to stricture on several independent grounds. A believer might even detect in it a
blasphemy: I ought to behave as if God existed in the hope
that if He does, I will be rewarded. Is it likely that I am going
to be saved as the result of a cold calculation, based not on
real worship but on the admission that God's existence is a
remote possibility and on a decision to act according to the
'just-in-case' logic of insurance? Pascal seems however to
anticipate implicitly this argument. His advice is that one
should start behaving as if God existed, i.e., should tame
one's own passions; but he expects that if a libertine – his
addressee – complies with the 'external' requirements of
Christian life, he will soon acquire a genuine faith and then
he will discover that in giving up his sinful habits he in fact
has lost nothing and that the currency he thought he had
risked was worthless paper.

Yet, even if a believer's objection may be thus dismissed, a
stubborn atheist will not be convinced. The efficacy of
Pascal's reasons depends on the psychological condition of
the recipient, in particular on his will to believe, his
hesitations about the rightness of his life style and his
readiness to admit that God's presence, without being
certain, has at least a degree of plausibility. An atheist
doggedly sticking by his unbelief would not be moved: in his
view God's existence has zero probability and all we have are
the pleasures of life, ephemeral though they be.

It needs stressing that Pascal's intention was not to
'prove' God's existence or to reinforce the existing arguments; he was willing to admit that the world, as our senses,
our science and our logic perceive it, does not reveal
unequivocally the hand of Providence. Nor is it likely that he
himself was actually led to his belief by the kind of wager he
recommended to his sceptical friends. He tried to show that
Christian faith, albeit risky, is much less risky than its
refusal and that, once accepted for practical reasons, it will
step by step develop into the real thing; a sceptic who has

decided to bet on God will soon notice how right he was not only in terms of the loss-and-gain calculation but in cognitive terms as well: all the desperate absurdities of human fate are going to make sense in the light of revelation.

In short, Pascal's insurance scheme clearly implies the principle *credo ut intelligam*. It leaves untouched the epistemological status of Christian beliefs. Pascal knew that. He never tried, as many theologians did, to convert faith into a second rate secular knowledge. He knew that profane Reason is powerless to cope with the 'problem of God' and that, strictly speaking, no such 'problem' exists, because God is not an unknown quantity in some equation we have to solve but a reality which appears to the believer in the act of worship, and no intellectual contrivance, however ingenious, can of its own power prompt us to such acts or to any acts whatever.

Conclusion: what comes first?

There is no idea behind which we could not, if we so wished, discover another one, and there is no human motivation which we could not, if we tried hard, consider the deceptive expression of another, allegedly more deeply seated, motivation. The distinction between what is deeper, more 'genuine', 'real', 'hidden', and what is merely a disguise, a mystifying form, a distorted translation, is established by the supreme philosophical fiat of anthropologists, psychologists, metaphysicians. Thinkers who are obsessed with the vision of a monistic order and who try to reduce all human behaviour patterns, all thoughts, and all reactions to one kind of motivation invariably succeed. We may decide, for instance, that human self-assertiveness ('will to power', striving for perfection, etc.) is a basic drive which dominates all behaviour patterns, including sexual ones, or we may carry out a reduction in the opposite direction; we may peremptorily state that all human ideas, social institutions and movements ultimately express conflicts of material interests or, on the contrary, that various conflicts of interest, not unlike various forms of human creativity, should be viewed as components of a grandiose effort of Spirit seeking the final reconciliation with itself. With a sufficient amount of ingenuity – and nobody could deny that the great monistically oriented philosophers, including philosophers disguised as anthropologists, psychiatrists, economists or historians, had it in abundance – any attempt to discover one all-ordering, all encompassing and all-explaining principle for the whole variety of cultural life-forms will yield irrefutable and thus true results. On the assumption that people can be, or that more often than not they actually are bound to be, unaware of their own motivations or of the genuine meaning of their acts, there are no imaginary let alone effectively known, facts which might prevent a stubborn monist from being always right, no matter how the fundamental principle of understanding is defined. Monistic reductions in general anthropology or 'historiosophy' are always successful and convincing; a Hegelian, a Freudian, a Marxist, an Adlerian are, each of them, safe from refutation as long as he is consistently immured in his dogma and does not try to soften it or to make concessions to common sense; his explanatory device will work for ever.

This applies to the vicissitudes of religious myths, symbols, rituals and beliefs. Considering their connections with all other areas of collective and individual life, considering obvious and innumerable examples of religious imagery and forms of worship being put to the service of all kinds of non-holy human interests, considering how their historical destinies have run parallel to changes in the secular aspects of civilization, it is fairly easy to jump from here to a general theory and to devise a reduction mechanism whereby the entire realm of religion will be granted the status of an instrument to satisfy other presumably genuine needs – social or psychological, cognitive or material. Such jumps are never logically justifiable and yet, once performed, they not only give the jumper the satisfaction of being possessed of a comprehensive theoretical understanding of the 'religious phenomenon' but they will be borne out by each successive example under scrutiny.

It is not my intention to discuss the presently available

variety of theoretical machinery: both because the topic is beyond the boundaries I have set for my essay and because the monistic versions of anthropological reduction seem to be much less in fashion nowadays than they used to be. My point is simply that all theoretical schemas of reduction, monistic or otherwise, are in no better an epistemological position than the theologians' efforts to make secular events intelligible in religious categories. Why should it be more plausible to say that mystical love is a derivation of worldly Eros than that the latter is a pale reflection of the all-embracing divine love out of which the universe was conceived? Is God an alienated man or rather is man God's self-alienation? Is the figure of God's son an imaginary sublimation of earthly sonship or rather its archetypal paradigm? Everything goes back to the same anxiety: is the world of our perception the ultimate reality which people have embellished with a non-existent 'meaning' according to their various psychological and social self-defence mechanisms, thus preventing themselves, by those artificial adornments, from seeing the world as it is? Is the eternal reality a dreamy fabrication of our yearning after security? Or is the world more like a screen through which we dimly perceive a meaning and an order different from that which rational investigation can provide us with? Is the very quest

---

For if life were questioned a thousand years and asked: 'Why live?' and if there were an answer, it could be no more than this: 'I live only to live!' And that is because Life is its own reason for being, springs from its own source, and goes on and on, without ever asking why – just because it is life.

Meister Eckhart, tr. R. B. Blakney

---

for security, far from being a phantasmagoric sublimation of the natural and universal fear of suffering, a sign of our share in the eternal sense-endowed order, of our status as meta-physical beings, a status we may almost, yet never entirely, forget? Does a phantom-God blur our vision of things or, on the contrary, does the world veil God from our sight?

Let us state again, in slightly different words, not what the answer is but what is the status of the question. The question, I was arguing, is not answerable without a *petitio principii* because each of the two colliding ways of seeing the world has its own rules of validity and each rejects the other's criteria. Unable to convince each other, the adherents of two incompatible notions can only try to compel the adversary to be as self-consistent as possible, that he may draw the ultimate conclusions from his own premises; this can be done if self-consistency, at least within limits, is admitted as a common rule.

The rationalist's world, a believer is never tired of arguing, is not a Cosmos, it displays no order and no meaning, it generates no good or evil, no purpose and no law. We have to face an indifferent chaos which produced us as aimlessly as it will eventually annihilate us; we have to accept that all human hopes and fears, all ecstatic joys and dreadful pains, all the creative torments of scholars, artists, saints and technicians are going to vanish forever without trace, engulfed in the wanton and boundless sea of chance. Consistent atheists have been ready to accept those conclusions; some, like Hume, with melancholy resignation, others, like Nietzsche, Sartre, Kafka, Camus, with the painful sense of a tragic conflict which would ever tear us asunder: the unbridgeable abyss between our search for meaning and the world as it is and is bound to remain. And yet most of those who – unlike the advocate of the gay and cosy atheism of the Enlightenment – were ready to stare at the icy desert of a godless world, had not given up the belief that something could be saved from the impersonal game of atoms. The 'something' was to be human dignity, the very ability fearlessly to face one's own freedom and to decree a meaning by the sheer act of will, in the full awareness that one was decreeing rather than discovering it in nature or in history. Whether Nietzsche was 'influenced' by the science of his time or simply used what he believed to be its inescapable consequences to support his philosophical preferences, is immaterial in this context; he was convinced (a point which his arch-expert, Karl Schlechta, strongly stressed) that science had definitively robbed the world, including human history, of sense, that God had abandoned the universe for ever and that no substitute for Him might be found. The dignity which enables us to accept the truth and to defy, by creative acts, the emptiness of Being, was to him the only way of carrying the burden of life without illusions. He failed to explain where the value of dignity came from, why it should not be another self-deception or why we may rely upon it rather than commit suicide or go mad, as he himself would subsequently do.

Nietzsche did not hesitate to assent to what great Christian teachers had always argued: the universe deserted by God is an absurd universe. Provided that the adjective 'absurd' may be used in a non-absurd way beyond the realm of grammar and that its etymology – *surdus*, deaf – is retained in its use, one might suspect such a saying of being tautologically true: a godless world is a world without God. It is, however, one of those pseudo-tautologies which people sometimes discover with a sudden joyful, or horrifying, feeling of revelation; here belong such discoveries as 'God is God' or *Cogito ergo sum*. And if the universe is really deaf, it does not matter at all whether or not I have the gift of speech: I *am* mute and my speech is an illusion, a game I play (*ludo*) with myself. *Nada*, *nihil*, nothing, is the last word and the last will of a vanishing God and of man who witnesses and accepts His departure. So spoke Job, David, Ecclesiastes, Pascal, Dostoyevski, Kierkegaard, and so spoke Lucretius, Schopenhauer, Nietzsche, Sartre, Camus, Céline and many others.

Those pious souls who are blissfully satisfied in their inherited certainty, never stirred by doubt, cannot find a source of comfort in the consistent atheist's avowal of nihilism. The latter would concede that the world as he sees it is not the abode of hilarity; why, it was not produced to make its denizens happy. His image of life makes understandable both the human condition and the reason why people seek an illusory escape from it into the realm of celestial justice.

And an atheist can now use the same weapon the believer employed when he cornered his opponent and forced him to accept the nihilst consequences of his axiom: he wants to compel the believer to be consistent. The believer should admit not only that he is unable to provide rational arguments in favour of his faith but moreover that he fails to explain the very content of his world view in rationally intelligible words: he cannot say how and why, on the premise of God's self-contained perfection, the world was created; how God is both the absolute Being and a person; how divine grace and the blind laws of nature co-exist and jointly form the rule of justice; why natural laws produce so much evil and suffering which serve no obvious purpose, etc. In short, he should admit that his entire perception of the world is based on an untestable trust in a Person whose very existence cannot be ascertained at the best and is self-contradictory at the worst. Besides, he may not deny that in his view men are not masters of their fate, that what they ought to or must not do has been arbitrarily decided by an unknown Lord whose orders allow for no appeal: thus they have to accept the status of slaves and to renounce their human dignity.

A believer's certainty, I was arguing, need not be shaken by these strictures. He may be ready to admit that his faith is an act of trust and of the feeling of participation in the divine order, not a scientific hypothesis. Not unlike a rationalist who can, within his *Weltanschauung*, encompass and explain the fact of religious faith, a believer, in his turn, knows how to comprehend and understand rationalism and atheism in terms of his belief. The rationalist's rules of acceptability, he would argue, are ultimately grounded on the usefulness of knowledge, notably on its ability to predict and to control natural phenomena; whatever is known in the realm of religious worship is demonstrably not useful in this sense and therefore, in accordance with those rules, is no knowledge at all. The rules of rationalism, once accepted, yield the cognitive results they were established to yield. But the perception of the world in terms of divinely guided order is equally consistent and provides the believer with an understanding which a rationalist simply refuses to be interested in. The believer's certainty admittedly cannot be expressed in a language which would meet the requirements of scientific discourse, and indeed the language of the Sacred is not a part or an extension of the everyday speech; it is understandable within the life of the Sacred, in acts of worship. The validity of the religious experience may be or even has to be rejected by a rationalist, as this experience does not fit into the conceptual framework he has built on his normative definition of knowledge; a believer is perfectly entitled not to bother about this very rejection. This is merely to rephrase what many religious teachers and thinkers have repeatedly argued; they do not pretend to have discovered God's presence in the way a hunter ascertains that an elephant was here by seeing its footprints, or an astronomer detects an unknown planet by calculating the perturbations of the visible ones. They believe that a world illuminated by faith is more understandable than a world without faith, or rather that it is not understandable at all except in the light of faith; they do not maintain that faith can be born from unprejudiced observation alone, if such a thing as unprejudiced observation is conceivable. Pascal went further than most, perhaps, in depicting the issue from the Christian standpoint. His position may be summed up briefly: there is a sense in which the basic tenets of faith – God, the union of mind and body, original sin – are absurd and yet the world image which excludes those tenets is even more absurd.

As to the time-honoured Promethean axiom holding that God's sway over the human race is a denial of man's dignity, this is a value judgement which is far from being more obvious than the opposite one. Hegel says (in the *Philosophy of History*) that man can respect himself only if he is aware of the higher being, whereas man's self-appointed promotion to the highest position implies a lack of self-respect. On this point Hegel says no more than the Christian tradition. Indeed, it may always be argued that if man, being aware of his contingent position in the universe, claims to be the supreme legislator in matters of good and evil, he has no cogent ground whatever for respecting himself or anything else, and that the very idea of dignity, if it is not a whimsical fancy, can be founded only in the authority of an indestructible Mind. To any anthropocentric notion of the world may be objected what the rationalists say about religious belief: that such a notion is nothing but an imaginary contrivance to compensate man's well-justified and depressing awareness of his own infirmity, frailty, uncertainty, finitude. Human dignity is not to be validated within a naturalistic concept of man. And so, the same either/or recurs time and again; the absence of God, when consistently upheld and thoroughly examined, spells the ruin of man in the sense that it demolishes or robs of meaning everything we have been used to think of as the essence of being human: the quest for truth, the distinction of good and evil, the claim to dignity, the claim to creating something that withstands the indifferent destructiveness of time.

Once again: even if the rationalist admits the dilemma 'either God or emptiness', he will still insist, and rightly so, that this offers no 'proofs' which might incite him to go over to the side of the believer. A believer may and ought to agree;

indeed, if he is consistent, he would say that the idea of 'proving one's faith' is a contradiction in terms. He knows that the appeal to religious experience may always be dismissed by a rationalist and relegated to the region of dreams.

So of course may be the idea of revelation. Gods have spoken to men and disclosed themselves in one way or another in all religions, yet revelation in a narrow sense, i.e., a well-defined and specific body of verbal messages which pass for God's word, is characteristic of the prophetic religions which emerged in the Mediterranean deserts. The concept of sacred texts or of divinely inspired and thus infallible books seems to be much less rigorous in the Buddhist and Hindu traditions, a difference which is obviously connected with the high degree of institutionalization in Judaic, Christian, and Islamic creeds. The stronger the institutionalized forms of religious worship, the greater the need for a strictly identifiable corpus of canonical scriptures, for a collection of indisputable and indubitable dogmas, and for an authority empowered to interpret them. In this respect the difference between 'West' and 'East' is striking, and within the Western tradition the Roman Catholic Church has obviously reached the highest degree of institutionalization of the divine word. And it has given a clear shape to the idea of continuity without which no religion can survive as a historically established entity. The very concept of the Church as a charismatic community implies its function as the reliable truth-keeper and truth-interpreter; if we have only a body of sacred books which each generation is supposed to become acquainted with, but no concept of the continuous growth of a tradition which is made valid by the sheer fact of being stored in the holy community, the Church either is useless or is no more than a secular organism helping individuals in their religious worries and duties. This is how many radicals of the Reformation argued; they attacked not a single corrupted

By no thinking can man come closer to the reality which is experienced by a believer in the embodied presence (*Leibhaftigkeit*) of God . . . The reality is in the world of worship and the Church. Revelation and God's word cannot be received privately. They acquire reality only through the presence of the Holy in an institution.

Karl Jaspers

Church but the idea of the Church as such; and so did their great nineteenth-century descendant Søren Kierkegaard. On the assumption that religion is about salvation, and that only individuals, not societies, churches or tribes, are saved and condemned, it might appear that the entire field of religious life is confined to the mysterious invisible communication between a personal conscience and God and that profane history (or history *tout court*, since sacred history, in this view, is not a history proper, not a cumulative process) generated nothing that would be relevant to the cause of salvation. By the mainstream of Christianity this approach was naturally suspected of the Manichean fallacy; it came close to the assertion that Nature itself, including our physical life, was irredeemably in the grip of Evil; this amounted to denying the concept of Incarnation whereby God had, as it were, sanctified the body, and indeed to suggesting that the very act of creation had been evil and could not have been performed by God, but only by His foe (the Cathars gave credence to this terrifying doctrine).

The biblical religions, except in the case of certain peripheral phenomena, did not separate Nature from Spirit along the axis dividing Evil from Good; they believed in the goodness, albeit relative and derivative, of the physical world, of profane history, of secular life; this attitude was confirmed in the Christian dogma of Incarnation, of the resurrection of the body and of the soul being the form of body. Therefore they were conceptually ready to work out the notion of the visible charismatic church which, being a worldly organism, is simultaneously the unerring guardian and the vehicle of divine gifts.

There is nothing that is supernatural in the whole system of our Redemption. Every part of it has its ground in the workings and powers of nature, and all our redemption is only nature set right, or made to be that which it ought to be. There is nothing that is supernatural, but God alone; everything beside Him is subject to the state of nature.

William Law (1686–1761)

The idea of the Church has to be mentioned in this context because it is relevant to the perception of truth in the realm of the Sacred, or rather it expresses in the most articulate manner what in all religions has been a persistent component of their truth-claims: the validating power of continuity.

The linking of truth with continuity has always been, not surprisingly, an outstandingly easy target of rationalist derision. In terms of this critique, it amounts to saying that something is true for no better reason than that it has been considered true for many generations or that some of our ancestors believed it was true. The truth-claims of institutionalized religious bodies were repeatedly accused of the most crude vicious circle: the revealed word has to be believed because the Church says it is true and what the Church says is true because its authority is based on Revelation (this dilemma was perhaps best illustrated in the old Jewish joke about two Chassidim disputing the excellence of their respective tsadiks; 'every Friday night', one of them says, 'God converses with our tsadik'; 'how do you know that?', the other asks; 'the tsadik himself told us so'; 'maybe he lied?', 'how dare you accuse of lying a man with whom God converses every Friday!').

Indeed, if continuity is conceived of as a criterion of truth in the normal sense of the word, the claims of religious bodies to be carriers of truth have to look absurd. But they do not seem at all absurd if we bear in mind the idea of validity which is specific to the realm of the Sacred. Since, as I have tried to show, religion is not a set of propositions but a way of life in which understanding, believing and commitment emerge together in a single act (something which is expressed with awkwardness in 'doctrinal' terms) and since people enter upon this way of life as a result of their actual initiation into communal worship, it seems natural that religious truth should be preserved and handed over in the continuity of collective experience. And, in religious life, to have seen the truth is to pledge loyalty to a Law which is both 'positive' and 'natural', since in the absolute mind there is no distinction between establishing the 'goal of life' for people and the technique for achieving it; the true and the good are identical and thus there is such a thing as a 'true goal' or a 'calling' of man. The expression 'to be in truth' makes sense in religious language, since to have found truth is not to have learnt certain theological statements but to have entered the path leading to ultimate deliverance. Jesus' saying that the truth will make us free does not mean that the mastery of technical skills will lead to a desirable result; for Him, and for all great religious teachers, people realize the nature of their bondage in the same act of illumination that includes the means of shaking it off and the understanding of the divinely ordained destiny of the world. By saying that Nirvana is the destruction of craving Buddha does not provide us with the 'definition' of a metaphysical entity but shows man's goal as it 'verily is'.

No philosophical speculation can perform this task. In spite of the claims of philosophical transcendentalism it is only by reference to the all-knowing and eternal mind that the convergence of goals and knowledge is attainable, whereas in secular life the 'is' and the 'ought to' are bound to be separated; they can only be 'mediated', to use Hegel's idiom, through that participation in the Sacred which reveals, however imperfectly, the infinite wisdom.

To be sure, it is not impossible to assent to certain 'statements' belonging to the doctrinal side of a religion and to accept them as true in the same sense as we accept without question many pieces of information, factual or theoretical. Such acts of assent simply do not belong to what we usually call religious belief; these 'statements' lie fallow, as it were, and have no significance as instruments of communion with the Sacred; our brain stores countless fragments of vitrified knowledge, connected to nothing, serving no purpose, having no value in our life, and there is no reason why some of them should not be theological in content. With religious faith they have little to do.

It would be utterly wrong to infer from the foregoing discussion that the conflict between the Reason of the Enlightenment and religious certitudes or, on a larger scale, between the Profane and the Sacred, may be in my view explained in terms of logical mistakes, conceptual confusion or misconceived ideas about borderlines between knowledge and faith. Such an approach would appear to me grotesquely inadequate. The conflict is cultural, not logical, and it is arguably rooted in the persistent, irreconcilable claims imposed on us by various forces within human nature. It is clearly less prominent in some civilizations than in others; it is hardly traceable or perhaps even absent in some historical periods; and its intensity seems to depend in part on the pace of change to which a given society is subject. (These are not strictly correlated, of course; theories of the 'secularization' which has overtaken our own civilization usually point out a number of independent variables which are at work in the process and can reinforce or weaken each other's impact; there is no way of grasping these forces in form of quantifiable vectors, let along of using those findings for reliable predictions.)

Sociological investigation is in any case beyond my present scope. I have wanted, rather, to speculate on that collision which no imaginable future civilization is likely to abolish. In addition to all the needs which are either directly related to, or functionally explainable by, our *conatus ad suum esse conservandum*, our aspiration for individual and collective survival, there are needs which cannot be explained (or explained away) in such terms and which we, appropriately or not, call religious.

I am of course only repeating or rephrasing an old tenet. Like all conjectural attempts to reach a 'definition' of man in cultural terms, it is bound to carry a speculative component and cannot be sufficiently grounded in historical or anthropological research; these might be suggestive, but cannot be conclusive. The sheer historical persistence of a phenomenon does not provide a persuasive basis for such a definition, which must be founded primarily on guesswork – work which can be dismissed as either useless or unfeasible or both. Whether it is deemed useless or not, depends on our hierarchy of importance. On some presuppositions about what is important it will inevitably be classed as useless, thus sharing the lot of the entire field of philosophy and of a major portion of the humanities. Whether it is deemed feasible or not again depends on epistemological restrictions which, I argued, are unavoidably arbitrary and value-loaded. Since time immemorial people have been asking, in one way or another, 'what are we?' and 'what is our life for?', and it hardly extinguishes their curiosity to say that it is forbidden by such or another philosophical school on the ground of its norms of meaningfulness. Religious mythologies have supplied them with answers and irrespective of the question whether or not and in what sense these answers were 'good', the very persistence of their concern is a matter of epistemological, and not merely anthropological, interest. It is unlikely that the strange obstinacy of this inquisitiveness could be plausibly explained by its 'functional' utility; neither are the answers provided by mythological traditions likely to be made intelligible this way. There is no understandable transition from everyday experience, from 'profane' fears, joys, pains and desires, to what makes up the core of religious life, of both its 'experimental' and conceptual aspects: the idea of the actual Infinitude, of Eternity, of the contingency of the world; the experience of mystical illumination; the very distinction between good and evil as different from corresponding distinctions in terms of law or of the pain-and-pleasure balance. There is no way that profane sight could have suggested the sacral framework for our perception. If religions could meet, as they have done throughout history, all secular needs – political, social or cognitive – this has only been possible on the condition that the Sacred enjoyed an autonomous authority and was not perceived as an instrument. This is, of course, almost universally recognized. Yet the explanation of this authority in Durkheimian or similar terms, heuristically useful though it may have been to anthropological inquiry, involves a conceptual leap which only philosophical premises, brought from elsewhere, may justify. To say that the Sacred is, ultimately, Society itself is neither equivalent to, nor may be inferred from, the proposition that various socially important norms and habits are maintained and obeyed in the form of sacral prescriptions. The former statement is not a sociological hypothesis but a kind of social metaphysics; it presupposes a mechanism whereby the Profane is converted into the Sacred, and such a mechanism, apart from being unobservable, cannot operate unless the Sacred is already present in social consciousness; in other words, the explanation stumbles against the same *petitio principii* of which Malinowski once accused Freud: it leaves the transition to a human from a pre-human society dependent on conditions which can only emerge in a human society already in existence. To say instead that the realm of the Sacred, however much it is at work in organizing other needs, is not functionally dependent on them, is not a testable hypothesis either, and though it avoids the circularity just mentioned, it too remains on the quaggy soil of metaphysics.

Another global interpretation in terms of *Lebensphiloso-phie* or of a radically naturalistic theory of behaviour suggests that the weakening of the inborn mechanism of inhibition in human species induced Nature to produce a substitute in the form of ethics supported by religious sanctions; the latter came about in order to guarantee the efficacy of this new artificial code of behaviour which had replaced the debilitated instincts, to reduce killing within the species and to assure readiness to risk danger in defending one's own tribe or family.

This line of inquiry seems to be unpromising and unreliable. If it were really the case that religions are ersatz-instincts manufactured by Nature's ingenious factory of survival gadgets, this should apply *par excellence* to the great universal religions which by their very success proved most efficient in performing the job. And so, we should assume that crucial tenets like the Christian demand that one should love one's enemies and Buddhism's utter contempt for a life that cannot be anything but misery, were invented, inconceivably, by evolution to help people in their struggle for survival. Moreover, if we can believe that, then we should admit that these very precepts had their equivalents in our pre-human or half-human ancestor, since their real meaning lay in their artificial reinforcement of certain hereditary abilities which had become decrepit as a result of the progress (or degeneration, whichever sounds better) of our species. This seems an astonishingly incredible hypothesis. If, on the other hand, we admitted a sort of Bergsonian distinction between 'static' and 'dynamic' religions, only the former being explicable in terms of natural evolution, then the latter, which include the great religions dividing among themselves most of the human race, would be either enemies of 'instinct' or at least would prevent us from defining culture in functional categories.

And indeed, even on the implausible assumption that the clash between the Sacred and the Profane is characteristic of some civilizations, including our own, and has not existed at all either in archaic or in Eastern religions, its persistence and the great variety of its manifestations make us naturally wonder: do we have to do with an accidental collision or rather with a fundamental conflict which might have remained latent here and there yet was bound to emerge as a result of the sheer growth in human abilities to master the world?

All the powers and dignities of this world are not only alien from God but hostile to him.

Tertullian, tr. H. Bettenson

The factual elements which are required to answer such a question would encompass the complete history of all religions, whereas its unavoidable speculative components must necessarily be derived from the ontology of culture. Therefore there is a sense in which the question is unanswerable; it shares this position with all the general problems belonging to the philosophy of history. They cannot be answered properly and have to be answered nonetheless.

We are, of course, familiar with the conflict in a form peculiar to the biblical religions and to Christianity above all, and it is mainly in Christian terms that it has been discussed for centuries. It is possible that Buddhist wisdom, or at least those variants of it which have stayed the closest to the original message, failed to develop, and in fact did not need, the distinction between the Sacred and the Profane as we know it, apart from the distinction between true and false goals. It is possible that the distinction failed to generate acute conflicts in many archaic religions where most of the profane activities had a sacral meaning and a well-defined place within a sacred order, while the very slow pace of social change allowed perhaps for the absorption of new phenomena into this order without great difficulties. In the civilization that has been developing out of Greek and Semitic roots for the last three millennia the conflict was bound to arise, and this not as the result of rivalry between the power of priests and that of secular lords – such rivalry being more a symptom than a cause – but because of inevitable alterations in mental and moral dispositions. We may think that the expansion of commerce and its growing role in human life brought about intellectual changes which fatefully eroded the mythological legacy, not only by breeding that scepticism which normally accompanies exposure to alien civilizations, foreign customs and foreign gods, but by nourishing rationalism as well. I use this word in a sense which preserves its etymological force (calculation, reckoning), meaning the habit of thinking in probabilistic terms, of measuring the value of knowledge in terms of its testable usefulness, of discarding beliefs having no potential for increasing the human drive to dominate the earth. The reason why it is unthinkable that our civilization might have developed without the widespread use of money is not only because of the obviously essential role money has played in stimulating technical progress but because it released an irresistible intellectual force by compelling human minds to think in terms of efficiency. Insofar as religious beliefs and customs can be serviceable in other areas and thus pragmatically 'good', rationalism is not intrinsically anti-religious. It is a foe of religion, however, to the extent that the latter tries to be what it is and to vindicate its own prerogatives, independent of its instrumental advantages. It is not possible to remove from religious worship a natural tendency to degrade the values of secular life and to make them relative and derivative, if not positively hostile to the genuine calling of man. A religious worship reduced to its secular utility and oblivious of its original function can survive for a time, no doubt, yet sooner or later its emptiness is bound to be exposed, the irrelevance of its form to its content will become apparent, its ambiguous life sustained by credit from a non-existent bank will come to end and the forgotten links with the Sacred will be resumed in another place, by other forms of religiosity.

The entire intellectual history of Christianity is a never-ending quest for a neat formula which might either assure the harmonious co-existence of the Profane with the Sacred or prevent the latter from being spoilt by the former; and it teems with recurring attempts to restore the pristine calling of Christianity from its adulteration, or simply its domination, by secular aims. The major trends in Christian history, irreconcilably inimical to each other, can be seen as various efforts to cope with this everlasting antagonism. Intellectually, though by no means practically, the conflict could be done away with by a theocratic doctrine completely subordinating secular life, in all its details, to religious prescriptions. Another solution consists in the ascetic separation of the Sacred from the world on the premise that profane life and profane history cannot contribute to, let alone fulfil the goals of, holy history: this may be done in extreme Manichean categories or in a theologically less risky way, as was attempted by certain sixteenth-century spirituals, by consistent Jansenists or by Kierkegaard. The most traditionally Catholic, hylomorphic philosophy, which grants the secular kingdom a relative autonomy under the surveillance of the Sacred, is another possible solution: it aims at a well-integrated harmony – not a separation or an armistice – of Heaven and Earth. So does, of course, the opposite ideal of the secular city which absorbs religious values within its goals (as in the young Hegel), makes them 'immanent', and consequently deprives them of properly religious meaning.

Each of these endeavours is plausibly explicable in historical terms and each might be intellectually satisfactory in the sense of suggesting rules which, if consistently followed in the society, would either result in the reconciliation of the two powers vying for ascendancy or eliminate the conflict. All of them however are utopian (in the current and original sense) because none of the models they offer can be implemented. Even the theocratic solution could produce only an appearance of order: it does not remove the conflict, it only applies totalitarian coercion to prevent it from being expressed. And those solutions which might be implemented are shaky, uncertain and provisional, like all the devices humanity invents to cope with its perennial predicaments. The clash between Heaven and Earth is real, which implies that each of them taken separately is real, at least as a cultural entity, and neither is a phantasm conceived in the other's imagination. This remark is not quite trivial or non-controversial, considering that the cultural reality of Heaven, i.e., its cultural independence or self-rootedness, is more often than not denied in general anthropological theories.

To an earth-bound eye the religious mind is like Ixion copulating with clouds and breeding monsters. A denizen of the eternal, divinely supervised order may say much the same of those who are deaf to the voice of God: they are attached only to what is short-lived and doomed to disappear in a moment; thus they are illusion-hunters, nothingness-seekers, and for this reason the only human community they are able to produce is bound to be based on greed for fictitious goods and on fear of mutual destruction. What is real or unreal to us is a matter of practical, rather than philosophical, commitment; the real is what people really crave for.

The unreal never is: the real never is not. This truth indeed
has been seen by those who can see the truth. Interwoven
in his creation, the Spirit is beyond destruction. No one
can bring to an end the Spirit which is everlasting.

For beyond time he dwells in these bodies, though these
bodies have an end in their time; but he remains
immeasurable, immortal. Therefore, great warrior, carry
on thy fight. Beyond the power of sword and fire, beyond
the power of waters and winds, the Spirit is everlasting,
omnipresent, never changing, never moving, ever One.

From: The Bhagavad Gita, *2. tr. J. Mascaró*

Index

Leszek Kolakowski was born in 1927 in Radom, Poland. He studied at Lódz University and at Warsaw University, where he took his D.Phil. in 1953 and later became Professor of the History of Philosophy. During the same period he also worked at the Institute of Philosophy of the Polish Academy of Sciences, and was editor-in-chief of the main philosophical journal in Poland. In March 1968 he was expelled from his university post by the Polish government for political reasons. He was Visiting Professor in the Department of Philosophy at McGill University, Montreal, in 1968–69, at the University of California at Berkeley in 1969–70, and at Yale University in 1975. From 1981 to 1994 he was Professor on the Committee of Social Thought at the University of Chicago. He is a member of All Souls College, Oxford, where he was Senior Research Fellow from 1970 until his retirement in 1995.

Leszek Kolakowski is the author of over thirty books. Those written in or translated into English include *Main Currents of Marxism* (3 vols., 1978); *Religion* (1982); *Bergson* (1984); *Metaphysical Horror* (1988); *The Presence of Myth* (1989); *Modernity on Endless Trial* (1995); *God Owes Us Nothing: A Brief Remark on Pascal's Religion and the Spirit of Jansenism* (1995) and *Freedom, Fame, Lying and Betrayal* (1999). He has written books in Polish, French and German, and translated philosophical texts from many different languages. He has also written short stories and plays.

He is a fellow of the British Academy, the Académie Universelle des Cultures, the Academia Europea and the Bayerische Academie der Künste; a Foreign Fellow of the American Academy of Arts and Sciences; and a member of the International Institute of Philosophy, the Pen Club, the Polish Academy of Sciences, and philosophical associations in Britain and Poland.

He has been widely honoured, and has received the Jurzykowski Prize (1969), the Friedenspreis des Deutschen Buchhandels (1977), the Prix Européen de l'Essai (1981), the Praemium Erasmianum (1982), the McArthur Fellowship (1983), the Jefferson Award (1986), the Prix Tocqueville (1993), the Premio Nonino (1997), the Prize of the Polish Pen Club (1988), and six doctorates *honoris causa*.